This general map of the Chatham area shows the extent of development towards the end of the 19th century.

CHATHAM PAST

An 18th-century view of the River Medway and Chatham dockyard. To the right can be seen the newly rebuilt parish church while further down the river a new warship is nearly ready for launching. In the foreground is the Gun Wharf and the building which now serves as 'The Command House'.

CHATHAM PAST

Philip MacDougall

Phillimore

1999

Published by
PHILLIMORE & CO. LTD.
Shopwyke Manor Barn, Chichester, West Sussex

ISBN 1 86077 121 1

Printed and bound in Great Britain by
BIDDLES LTD.
Guildford, Surrey

To Marcus, Ewan and Elspeth
all of whom were born in Chatham

Contents

List of Illustrations

Frontispiece: Eighteenth-century view of the River Medway

Acknowledgements

A great number of people have helped me over the years, all of them providing small snippets of information that have helped in putting together this story of Chatham. Among those who have especially helped—sometimes unknowingly—are Colin Allen, Bruce Aubry, Les Collins, Peter Dawson, Sylvia Field, Brian Joyce, the Phillips family, Dave Turner and Mavis Waters. In addition, mention must be made of the staff of Chatham Library, the Medway Archives Office and the the Medway Heritage Centre for their patience and helpfulness in all matters connected with my attempts at unearthing useful and interesting material. To all these, and many others, I am most grateful.

Introduction

Some readers may consider that I have taken an unusual approach in writing this history of Chatham. Although the arrangement is primarily chronological, I concede that I have begun well forward in time—the year 1568 to be exact. The frequently adopted traditional approach is to start with the odd dinosaur and then develop a discussion on the presence of Neanderthal man. This I have chosen not to do. I am not denying that dinosaurs probably roamed that patch of land which has since acquired the name Chatham, but such conjectural evidence does not really add much to the story of the later town. On the other hand, the year 1568 would appear to represent the birth of that same town. In that year a naval dockyard was established on the river bank just beneath St Mary's Church. From this point on, Chatham quickly developed into a thriving, bustling township. I have not ignored what went before, however. The medieval village is given fair treatment while the Romans and Saxons are left to a later chapter. Given that much of the evidence relating to a Roman and Saxon occupation of the area was uncovered during the building of the Great Lines, I have connected this aspect of Chatham's history to that same event. Furthermore, it allows the book to take an unusual perspective, considering the resulting archaeological finds not so much from a modern viewpoint, but through the eyes of those who lived at the time.

One other thing. Having already written a book on the history of the dockyard, I have pointedly avoided making too many references to the yard. But it has to be included—it is integral to this history of the town. Only on occasion, however, do I enter through the gates of the yard. This is the story of Chatham and its people. Many of them, of course, worked in the dockyard. If any reader desires to follow these same individuals into the yard, then I am sure their thirst will be satisfied by my own books on that subject. On occasions where the yard is mentioned, though, then I am adding to my previous books—repetition has been avoided. Indeed, much of what is included about the dockyard is new evidence—uncovered by myself or others.

PHILIP MACDOUGALL, Ph.D.

December 1999

One

On the Eve of Change

❖

I have not hitherto at any time, read any memorable thing recorded in historie touching Chetham it selfe …

William Lambarde (1570)

The year 1568 must be regarded as one of incredible importance for the area of North Kent known as Chatham. It was during this particular year that a government naval dockyard was first established on the banks of the River Medway, an event that inflicted massive and irrevocable change upon the lives of all those who lived in the area. From being resident in a quiet, unassuming backwater, these early inhabitants of Chatham found themselves uncompromisingly dominated by one of the most important industrial-military complexes found anywhere in the world. While some undoubtedly benefited, others must have suffered immensely from this sudden change in the quality of their lives. Given that there are few detailed historical records for this period, the best that can be achieved is a general description of pre-industrial Chatham village. From this, it is possible to decide the nature of this uninvited invasion and how seriously it influenced the everyday lives of those who had long seen Chatham as their village.

First and foremost there was a massive population increase. In 1568, Chatham had about 200 people living within its boundaries. In the space of a few years this number more than trebled. At first, the majority would have been employed in constructing the new yard. The most important tasks carried out were those of digging a mast pond and the building of storehouses and forges, together with the sinking of a number of saw pits. Furthermore, a 370ft. unloading wharf was built in 1580 while a dry dock was completed during the following year. All these structures were of timber, the new dockyard initially requiring a large number of sawyers, housecarpenters and labourers. As the yard took shape, the composition of the work force began to alter quite dramatically. Instead of a need for those possessing ordinary building skills, the requirement was for shipwrights, caulkers, mast makers and anchor smiths. Some would have been recruited from Woolwich and Deptford, the other naval dockyard towns of North Kent. The majority, however, were drawn from further afield, turning the tiny village of Chatham into a large cosmopolitan community that represented the four corners of the realm.

Doubtless, the young and able-bodied of Chatham village would have benefited. Although none would have possessed shipbuilding skills, they could certainly have undertaken various unskilled tasks associated with running a dockyard. The least ambitious could enter as labourers, while others

1 In earlier times, instead of Mountbatten House, this view across the riverside gardens would have been dominated by the village mill and mill pond, both located within the wider grassed area.

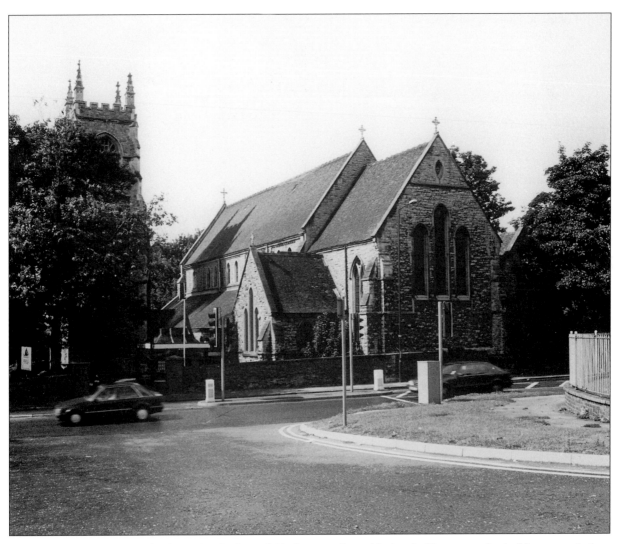

2 Providing a focal point for the medieval village of Chatham was the parish church. The present-day building, extensively rebuilt, bears little outward resemblance to its Norman predecessor.

might seek employment as a teamster (driving the cart horses used in shifting large objects), scavelman (responsible for cleaning and draining the dock) or sawyer. Beyond doubt, their employment opportunities were greatly enhanced by the arrival of the dockyard. Prior to this time, only a limited range of work opportunities existed within the village. Most people would have formed part of the agricultural labour force employed on the vast expanse of wheat and barley growing fields that stretched right across Chatham from the edge of St Mary's Island in the north to Luton in the south. Additional crops might well have included

peas, beans and oats. While some of it was retained for local consumption, vast amounts were shipped to London, the resulting payments making the 16th-century village relatively wealthy.

Part of the wheat crop retained for local consumption would have been taken to the village mill for grinding into flour. The mill itself has a very long history, going back as far as Saxon times. It was a large timber building that stood immediately alongside a mill pond fed from the waters of the old Bourne. Through the regulation of water by floodgates and sluices the miller was able to control the head of water, so producing sufficient power to turn the water wheel and grinding stones. From early maps, it is clear that the mill stood on the present-day site of Riverside Gardens, with the mill pond stretching out towards the library car park.

A further section of the population engaged in farm work were those involved in animal husbandry, the village possessing a number of animals that were kept for meat and other by-products. Sheep, for instance, kept for both meat and wool, were grazed on the marshes, this being the low-lying ground close to the river. Although adding to the wealth of the village, it was this area of land that also introduced a certain unhealthiness, the fresh-water marshlands harbouring malaria-carrying mosquitoes. A problem more frequently associated with the nearby Hoo Peninsula, there can be little doubt that the pre-industrial village of Chatham would have been plagued by these tiny insects that were capable of incubating then spreading the debilitating illness known as 'ague' or 'marsh fever'. Although a form of malaria, ague is an English strain of the disease and one much less virulent than might be found in the tropics. Those who contracted the disease would rarely die, only being incapacitated for a number of weeks. The real danger lay elsewhere. If, during the convalescent period and while still weak, they contracted some further illness, then death might become a real possibility. Furthermore, in the period immediately preceding the establishment of the dockyard, the village of Chatham was in the midst of a serious outbreak of the disease resulting from a number of extremely warm summers that had occurred during the three-year period 1566 to 1568. Such summers considerably aided the spread of the disease, the malaria-carrying female *anopheline* mosquito breeding abundantly on the stagnant marsh pools.

Once again, the construction of a dockyard at Chatham may have brought an advantage. As the yard expanded, much of the marshland along the river's edge was carefully drained and then incorporated into it. Certainly there is little evidence of malaria proving a problem for the industrial work force that lived in Chatham. On the other hand, the hot summer of 1568 saw a total of 15 deaths recorded in the burial register of St Mary's Church. Compared with the average for the next 20 years, this was an extremely high figure.[1]

3 Within the church of St Mary's, features dating back to the earlier medieval building are still clearly visible. Of particular significance is the zig-zag stonework around this 12th-century door.

As well as agricultural workers, whether employed on the surrounding fields or marshlands, the pre-industrial village also gave employment to a number of fishermen. For the most part, they would have lived close to the river shore and immediately below the parish church of St Mary's. A cluster of cottages existed here, fishermen themselves employing a number of small sail boats for the purpose of gathering the rich harvest of smelt, white bait, herring and even salmon which were once found in the river.

4 Evidence of a 14th-century reconstruction of the church can be seen in these foliage capitals that support a characteristic pointed arch.

Others dredged for oysters. Unfortunately for them, this was a less predictable occupation, the number of oysters being seriously depleted during the severe winter of 1564/5, part of the Medway freezing over during the months of December and January.

Beyond fishing and farming, there appears to have been a small range of additional occupations available to those who lived in the medieval village. We already know, for instance, that there must have been a miller (and probably an assistant apprentice) to keep the mill working, while a smith, baker and a few other artisans were likely to have found useful employment in the village. Evidence from elsewhere also suggests that a number of merchants used the area as a base. During the reign of Edward I, the hundred rolls,

which were compiled by special commissioners, indicate that two merchants traded out of the village, taking 'their ships laden with wool out of the port'.[2] By the beginning of the 16th century, trading still appears to have had a certain importance, a number of storehouses having been erected along the banks of the Medway.[3]

A further clue as to how some of the villagers of Chatham might have been employed comes from the surnames they possessed. Too much stress can be placed on this as an accurate source of information, as the origin of any name might go back several generations. As a result, the earliest known Chatham names, contained in a list of those who gave support to the Jack Cade rebellion of 1450, may tell us little about the trades followed by those particular individuals. On the other hand, geographical mobility was extremely limited and any one family would normally have remained within the same village for numerous decades. If these names were bestowed upon ancestors who had previously lived in the village, then they can certainly be used as a signpost indicating the tasks that some of the villagers had once undertaken (and possibly continued). Among the occupations noted in these names was that of barrel maker (Simon Couper), pedler (Johes Chapman), shoeing smith (Ricus Marchall), hide worker (Johes Pylcher), ropemaker (Rogus Roper), rabbit keeper (Willis Warner), and wood cutter (Robtus Wodear).[4]

Turning to the subject of land ownership, it is clear that much of the area surrounding the pre-industrial village was still held as part of the ancient manor. By 1568, the Manor of Chatham had fallen into the hands of Francis Barneham and Stephen Slanie, who had purchased it two years earlier. It is unlikely that either of them would have lived in the manor house, the largest and oldest of the secular buildings belonging to the village. Instead, this particular building, which was of timber construction and which once stood on the site of the modern-day High Street, would have been occupied by a steward who would, together with the reeve, oversee the affairs of the manor. Immediately around the manor house stood the demesne land, a large area of ground directly farmed by those in the manor house, as opposed to the majority of the land which was leased to a number of tenant farmers.

Prior to the purchase of the manor by Barneham and Slanie, it had been in the possession of Thomas Lord Wentworth. He, in turn, had acquired the manor through inheritance, being a descendant of Giles de Badlesmere who, during the 14th century, had received the manor from Edward III. However, the history of the manor can be traced back much further, to Domesday Book of 1086 which says a great deal about the manor and village in earlier times. According to this massive survey of property entitlement, carried out by William the Conqueror for purposes of taxation, the Manor of Chatham had formerly been in the possession of the defeated King Harold. Following his death at the Battle of Hastings, it had been given to William's half-brother, Odo, the Bishop of Bayeux. In fact, both Harold and Odo, successively, had held the majority of manors in Kent, with Chatham one of many. Because of his vast landholdings, Odo was in no position to concern himself with the direct management of these lands, choosing to lease the tenancy of Chatham to Robert Latin, one of his liegemen. As regards the manor itself, Domesday Book goes on to state that it contained about 1,600 acres of land and a further 20 acres of meadow and a small area of woodland. The manor also included the previously mentioned water mill (from which the owner of the manor took a proportion of all corn ground), a small church and six fisheries. For his part, Robert Latin held 600 acres of the available farm land in demsesne, with 37 serfs (included in the rent he paid to Odo) who undertook much of the farm work. The manor was stated to have had a taxable value of £12 under Harold while in 1086 it was assessed at £35. This much enhanced value, a factor that was out of step with many of the adjoining manors (such as those of Gillingham and Milton), may have been the result of an improvement programme carried out by the leaseholder, with Robert Latin possibly ordering some of the marshland to be drained, and converting it into pasture or meadowland for sheep and cattle. One other piece of information that dates back to this period of time relates to the reeve. He was the individual who served as a kind of foreman, toiling alongside those who worked on the demesne lands of the manor. Whereas a steward was of high status and might have lived in the manor house, the reeve was of low status and was appointed from among the villagers. The reeve of Chatham Manor in the 1090s, shortly after the compilation of Domesday Book, was a certain Aelwin Latimer.[5]

5 This font, possibly dating to the 14th-century rebuilding of the church, provides a further indicator of how the medieval church might have appeared to the earlier inhabitants of Chatham.

After 1086, the size of the manor and its attendant lands had been considerably reduced. At the time of compiling Domesday Book, Waldeslade had been accounted part of the Manor of Chatham. During the 13th century, however, Waldeslade had passed into the hands of the Leybourne family, with Henry de Leybourne, in the fourth year of Edward II's reign, obtaining a charter of free warren for lands in Waldeslade, Lidsing and Shawstead. A further division of land took place upon the death of Giles de Badlesmere, who possessed the manor during the reign of Edward III. To ensure that his sisters were not penniless, he had allowed some sixty acres of land to be detached and inherited by them. This land, which carried the name Snodhurst, was on the

ROBERT DE EYDA 1285
WILLIAM DE BORDENNE 1286
HENRY DE OPEGHERCHE circa 1293
NICHOLAS DE CHARTHAM before
HENRY DE APVLDREFELDE 1316
ROGER DE NEWENTON 1319
ROGER DE WY 1332
THOMAS RANDOLPH 1333
IOHN ATTE WELLE 1339
HENRY DAVYNGTON 1349
IOHN DE IRFORD 1349
PETER DE FARLEGHE 1361
IOHN DE GRAVENEY 1362
IOHN FARLEGH 1370
HENRY DE LONDON 1393
STEPHEN GRAY 1395
IOHN MARCHAVNT 1396
IOHN WHYTRESHAM 1423
THOMAS VINCENT 1444

6 Offering further clear evidence that the church is of a very early date is this list of past vicars fixed to the wall of the building. St Mary's no longer performs its original function, having become a heritage centre for the Medway area.

edge of Chatham and close to its border with Rochester. By 1568, Snodhurst was no longer independently owned, having been taken into Great Delce Manor. As for the Manor of Waldeslade, this had long ceased to be in the hands of the Leybourne family, having passed through a number of different owners that included the Priory of Chiltern Langley in Hertfordshire. The owner in 1568 was a London goldsmith named John Mabbe.

An even earlier loss of manor lands had occurred during the reign of Henry I, when Robert de Crevequer, whose father had acquired the manor upon Odo's fall from grace (the Bishop leading a rebellion against the King), allowed 30 acres of land to Leeds Priory. In fact, Robert de Crevequer was the founder of this priory, permitting it to be built on lands near Maidstone that he also owned. Included in the 30-acre gift from the Manor of Chatham were all benefits from the parish church. Possibly, Robert de Crevequer was also responsible for the rebuilding of this church. At the time of Domesday Book, reference is made to the existence of a church within the manor, but this would have been a small timber structure built by the Saxons. The Normans, on the other hand, entered into a massive church-building programme that did not begin until after the Domesday assessment. As such, de Crevequer is an obvious candidate for overseeing its reconstruction, ensuring that the new building, which may then have first acquired the name St Mary's, was of solid stone construction. While little of this original church now exists, it is fairly certain that it was of cruciform shape with a tower situated at its western end. The subsequent re-building of the church as a result of a fire in the early 14th century obscures our knowledge of that first stone church in Chatham.

Having acquired authority over the church, the prior of Leeds had the right to appoint priests to the parish, these normally drawn from among the canons of the priory. It would have been only fair then, for the priory to take responsibility for the upkeep of the church, especially in view of the wealth it took from both the 30 acres of land and individual offerings made by those who attended services at the church, but in 1316, when it became necessary to rebuild the church as a result of fire, it was resolved by the prior that the entire expense should fall upon the villagers. Despite help from Thomas de Woldeham, the Bishop of Rochester, who willed a 10-shilling donation, the task of rebuilding the church was quite beyond the villagers. As a result, the church was still unfinished by the middle of the century, with the Pope eventually coming to their assistance. In 1352, he issued a letter of indulgence, and this encouraged outside help by allowing anyone who made a financial donation to be remitted a year and 40 days of pennance. Once again, we know little of the detail of this building, for the present-day church, despite its medieval appearance, has since undergone two further rebuildings. However, the church completed in the 14th century would have adopted the Decorated style with the carved work, including an impressive sedilia and a shrine to the Virgin Mary, commanding considerable attention.

7 A second religious building that also serves as a reminder of Chatham's pre-dockyard past is St Bartholomew's Hospital Chapel, which is located in the High Street. The remaining building only hints at its early origins, the chapel having been heavily restored by Gilbert Scott during the 19th century.

As well as contributing little to the rebuilding and upkeep of the church, the priory was subsequently accused of deliberate deception in order to maximise donations to the church, this money then going directly into the coffers of the priory. The man who made this allegation was William Lambarde. In his impressive topographical study, *Perambulation of Kent*, which was published two years after the founding of the dockyard, he tells of a belief that either the priors or a church clerk had started a rumour claiming miracles had taken place around the church shrine. To this, so it was added, the Virgin Mary herself had walked the highways and byways of the area. As proof of this, her tracks could still be followed, for they had remained for 'ever after a greene path'. Lambarde was scathing in his dismissal of such claims, indicating 'that our Ladies path was some such green trace of grasse, as we daily behold in the fields'.[6] By Lambarde's time, not only was

the shrine much defaced but the monasteries and priories of Roman Catholicism had been dissolved, with much of their wealth falling into the hands of Henry VIII. As far as the church and lands of Chatham were concerned, these had passed over to the newly created dean and chapter of Rochester Cathedral, a situation that still existed in 1568.

Two further areas of land were also connected with the dean and chapter of Rochester, one through ownership and the other a result of patronage. Since the Dissolution, lands belonging to Shawstead Manor (which consisted of woodlands to the south), together with half of Lidsing (of which this part was then accounted to be within Chatham), had also come into their possession. Prior to the Dissolution, this same land had been in the possession of the priory, the priors of Rochester having themselves acquired the manor in 1376, it being granted to them at the yearly rent of 22 marks for ever. The owners of the Manor of Shawstead and the moiety of Lidsing at that time had been Robert Belknapp and his wife Amy.[7] The other piece of land connected with the dean and chapter stood at the western extremity of the parish at a point close to where it adjoins Rochester. Here, in 1078, Bishop Gundulf of Rochester acquired land for a lazar (or hospital that specialised in the care of those with leprosy). Named after St Bartholomew, the institution consisted primarily of a large hall and chapel, the south wall of the present-day chapel seemingly all that remains (above ground) of this ancient institution.[8] Within the hall of the hospital, lepers were cared for by the monks of the priory. From the time of its foundation, the poor brethren of St Bartholomew's Hospital received weekly and daily allowances of provisions from the priory together with all offerings made to the altar of St James and St Giles within the cathedral. This, together with more occasional donations, is in sharp contrast to the support given by the priors of Leeds to the parish church that lay within their possession. However, by 1568 the hospital was not in particularly good condition. Lambarde described it as 'yet a poor shewe of that decaied Hospitall of Saint Bartilmew'.[9] It would appear that, upon having come under the patronage of the dean and chapter, the hospital had fared less well than when dependent on the priory.

In completing this short survey of land ownership in Chatham, reference has yet to be made to two additional pieces of land which were in the possession of the nearby Manors of West Court and Horsted. In the case of Horsted, primarily in Rochester but straddling the boundary between Rochester and Chatham, the owner in 1568 was Sir Richard Lee, described as a citizen and grocer of London. As for West Court Manor,

which extended across Brompton and into the northern part of Chatham, the owner was Sir Nicholas Leveson of Whorne's Place in Cookstone, who had acquired the manor through family inheritance.

In virtually all cases, these land owners or their successors were also to benefit from the establishment of the dockyard. Those, such as Barneham and Slanie, who possessed land near the river, were able to lease and eventually sell land to the navy, while others who had land further inland were eventually to see demands placed upon it for purposes of house building. Even those further afield, such as the owner of Shawstead, would benefit, Shawstead manor possessing something that was in great demand: timber from the woods, a most important raw material that was equally required by both the dockyard (for purposes of shipbuilding) and those intending to build houses.

Despite the financial rewards, with most people appearing to gain from the establishment of a naval dockyard at Chatham, there were a number of drawbacks. In fact, there were considerable disadvantages that were to be shared by all who actually lived in Chatham. As the town grew, unrestricted house building and overcrowding were the natural result. In turn, this brought disease and death, Chatham soon having a death rate that was among the highest in the country. Most certainly the quality of life had changed, the inhabitants of the village exchanging good health for an enhancement of their wealth. The only ones who made unreserved gains were the absent landlords whose lands gained in value while they never had to set foot in the sprawling dirty township that Chatham was about to become.

Two

A Dock Furnished for the Finest Fleet

The charge of the Building to be made at Chatham, viz. the Dock, Wharfs, Brick work and storehouses will amount to an estimated £4000.

Report on the building of a second dockyard at Chatham (1611)

The decision to establish a naval dockyard at Chatham was not simply a capricious one. The earlier part of the 16th century had witnessed an increasing amount of naval activity, with the river at Chatham becoming an important anchorage. Among the more notable advantages of the Medway, apart from its proximity to London and a closeness to the North Sea, was that it provided sufficient space to accommodate the entire Tudor navy. Furthermore, once ships were at their moorings, there were few winds that could endanger them. Admiral Monson, writing in the early 17th century, made it clear that he believed the Medway to be superior to any other naval port. Of the anchorage at Chatham, he declared succinctly that it was 'so safe and secure a port for the ships to ride in that his Majesty's may better ride with a hawser at Chatham than with a cable at Portsmouth'.[1]

8 The origins of Chatham dockyard lie in the value of the Medway as a safe anchorage. This 18th-century view of the river shows a number of warships lying off the dockyard.

9 The first dockyard to be built at Chatham, which dates to 1568, was constructed upon land that lay immediately beneath the parish church. Today, this same area is occupied by Lloyd's Insurance Company.

It seems likely that the Navy first began using the Medway in 1547 when the grand sum of 13s. 4d. was paid by the Treasurer of the Navy for the use of storehouses at 'Jillyngham'. From then on, the annual statement of accounts, as presented to the Exchequer, show the continued payment of rents, with the amounts steadily rising as the demand for storehouses increased. By the year 1561, the cost to the Exchequer had more than quadrupled: 'Also paide by the said Accomptants for the rentes and hyer of Storehouses for thye storage of parte of the said provisions viz. at Deptford Strand 105s. Jillingham 60s.   5d. Colne 100s.'[2]

The question arises as to exactly where these storehouses might have been and who originally built them. Neither question can be answered with any certainty. It would be wrong, for instance, to jump to the seemingly obvious conclusion that the storehouses were all located close to the river at 'Jillyngham'. The subsequent construction of the dockyard at Chatham, combined with the use of Chatham Reach (rather than Gillingham Reach) as the most favoured stretch for the mooring of warships, would suggest that many of these storehouses lay within the parish of Chatham. Perhaps only the first of the rented storehouses was located in 'Jillingham', with that name subsequently used as shorthand for all Medway storehouses irrespective of their location. Frederick Cull, in his indispensable paper on the subject, suggests that the majority of these stores were probably located 'on the site of the former gunwharf and probably near its southern extremity'.[3] As to their origin, these storehouses may have been connected with merchant traders who had been using the port since the late 13th century.

The increasing value placed upon the Medway as a naval anchorage is amply demonstrated by two sets of orders from the year 1550. In June the Lord High Admiral was informed

> that the Kinges shipps shulde be harborowed in Jillingham Water, saving those that be at Portsmouth, to remaigne there till the yere be further spent, for avoiding of all inconveniencies, and that all masters of shippes, gonners and pursers be discharged except a convenient nombre, till the danger of the yere be past, and afterwards to be ordred as it hath been accustomed in time of peace.[4]

A few months later the privy council gave instructions for the writing of

> A lettre to the Lord High Admirall to remove the King's Majesties Shippes from Portsmouth to Gillyngeham Water wheare he shall take order that they may be calked and grounded, with commandements to take such souldeours as be of the Kinges presently in Sussex and on the sea costes to furnishe them for the more sure conduct of them through the Narrow Seas.[5]

It will be noted that the second of these instructions required a specific task—that of caulking. This was to ensure that the hulls belonging to these ships were still completely watertight, with skilled caulkers having to be employed in driving fresh oakum (once old oakum had been removed) into the seams between the planks that

10 As the dockyard gained in importance, becoming the nation's most important naval arsenal, it was necessary to provide for its defence. This resulted in the decision to build Upnor Castle.

made up the hulls. On completion, the hull had to be coated with hot melted pitch to prevent rotting. Although the process of caulking is best undertaken in dry dock, such a facility is not essential. Instead, these vessels, upon entering Chatham Reach, would have been deliberately beached so that the revealed hull could be worked upon. Once caulked and tarred, each vessel would be floated upon the next convenient high tide. For the successful completion of this task, the various rented storehouses would have been required to disgorge the necessary materials, mainly tar and picked oakum. In addition, the ships would need to be supplied with any short-fall in their own stores, with food, rope, canvas and other essential items brought out of the warehouses and taken over to the ships at anchor.

As the importance of the Chatham anchorage increased, so attention had to be given to other matters. First and foremost, there was a need to defend the fleet from enemy attack. Initially this involved the positioning of a bulwark (or battery of guns) at Sheerness, undertaken in 1551. The defences of the Medway were subsequently strengthened by the addition of a castle at Upnor, with orders for its construction given in 1560.[6] Of more direct importance to the future dockyard at Chatham was the expenditure in 1567 of £1,075 on ship repair work and related facilities. Included in this sum was rent for a newly acquired house to be used by officers overseeing the work of maintaining and repairing warships. In addition, some of this money was used for the digging out of a mast pond that could be used for the underwater storage of mast timbers.[7] However, it is unlikely that the mast pond would have been completed until the following year.

Eventually, then, we arrive at the momentous year of 1568. With the mast pond available, together with an anchor forge that also came into use during that year, a future dockyard was beginning to take shape. That this particular year can be nominated as the one that witnessed the actual establishment of Chatham dockyard is the result of a seemingly minor event, the purchase of a flag. However, this was no insignificant piece of cloth. Instead, it was the flag of St George and used to summon the workforce each morning. By raising this insignia, a clear and simple message was broadcast: a new naval dockyard had been established.

Confusingly, the dockyard as established in 1568 was not part of that area currently delineated as 'the historic dockyard'. Instead, it was further up-river and sited on land that is now occupied by the Lloyd's Insurance Company. This, of course, would make sense if the original storehouses, which continued to be used in this period, were also located here. Another building of significance was Hill House. Lying to the north of the dockyard (and about 50 yards beyond St Mary's Church), it was the building which had been rented a year earlier for the use of senior staff. By 1581 accounts reveal this substantial brick building to be under general renovation. Presumably, at that time it was being prepared as a residence for Matthew Baker, the nation's senior master shipwright.[8] It was his task to oversee much of the work undertaken in the royal dockyards, this necessitating frequent visits to Chatham. At the same time he had responsibility for work undertaken in the two other Kentish yards, those of Woolwich and Deptford.

Apart from the mast pond and smithery, the dockyard soon acquired a number of additional facilities. In the first decade of its existence, with land added in 1571 and 1575, a number of temporary workshops and stores must have been constructed. Generally, though, the work of maintaining and repairing ships was undertaken within the anchorage, gangs of shipwrights and other artisans rowing out to one or other of the ships each morning. By 1575, 120 shipwrights were employed. These, however, were not part of any permanent establishment. Instead, they were employed only for as long as ships were needed to meet the danger of foreign invasion. As a result, the numbers

employed would sharply fluctuate between seasons and from year to year.

A series of more permanent structures were added to the yard during the second decade of its existence. In particular, the year 1581 saw a considerable expenditure, with a series of storehouses, a dry dock and wharf all allowed for in that year's estimates. The purpose of the wharf, which was 378ft. in length, was primarily that of off-loading guns and other items of movable equipment from vessels that were either to winter in the Medway or were about to have essential repair work carried out. It is recorded that construction of the wharf was undertaken at a cost of five shillings a foot.[9] Positioned at the end of this wharf was a crane capable of carrying loads of up to three tons and which would have been powered by dockyard labourers working a treadwheel. The dry dock was primarily intended for various galleys that belonged to the Elizabethan navy and were used for towing larger vessels when not under sail. It was originally constructed with an earthen entrance that had to be laboriously broken up every time a vessel entered or left the dock. Although this was the normal procedure in use at other dockyards, the system had some rather obvious drawbacks. Shortly after its construction, therefore, it received the novel addition of a pair of flood gates.

Evidence of the not inconsiderable importance of Chatham dockyard and its adjoining anchorage is the decision by Queen Elizabeth to view ships in the Medway on at least two occasions. Her first visit to Chatham, made in September 1573, was fairly brief. However, a second visit, made nine years later, was a little more thorough and was recorded by Raphael Holinshed in his *Chronicles*:

> Queen Elizabeth having determined to accompany the Duke of Anjou [who sought the hand of the Queen in marriage] to the seaside, travelled with her court and lodged for the night in Rochester, and stayed the next day after inspecting the Queen's ships; Her Majestie shewed him all her great ships which were in that place, into most whereof his Highness and the Prince and Lords of his traine entered not without great admiration of the French Lords and Gentlemen, who confessed that of good right the Queene of England was reported to be Ladie of the Seas.[10]

Another who visited Chatham during these years was Sir John Hawkins. As Treasurer of the Navy, he played a crucial role in restructuring England's maritime arm, so placing it in a position to defeat the Spanish invasion attempt of 1588. As Treasurer, he not only came to Chatham to oversee the general defences of the area but he also took responsibility for laying down permanent moorings in the river. This was in 1578. At that time, the Medway having become a significant harbour, vessels had simply anchored anywhere in the river and were not necessarily directed to any particular area of safety. This changed upon the laying down of moorings, as these would only be placed in positions which had been previously surveyed. It also ensured that vessels were more carefully separated, with some moorings set aside for the very largest vessels.

Following victory over the Spanish Armada, Hawkins gave thought to the needs of both the ordinary seaman who had borne the brunt of the fighting and the shipwrights who had built and maintained the warships. For this reason he set up two charitable institutions, both of which were located in Chatham. The first of these was a pension scheme intended 'for the perpetual relief of such mariners, shipwrights and seafaring men' hurt or maimed while in government service. It was, in fact, one of the forerunners of the welfare state. All seamen and shipwrights employed in royal dockyards paid a small amount into the fund and, should an injury be later sustained, were allowed a pension for the period of incapacitation. All monies received for the fund were placed in a small opening at the top of a large oak chest that was probably kept, to begin with, at Hill House. Later, it was transferred to offices within the dockyard itself. Unfortunately, the scheme never worked as well as it might have done, the foundation earning for itself an unenviable reputation for corruption and mismanagement. Certainly, those responsible for directing the affairs of the Chest seemed to have used its monies for their own purposes. One such offender was Robert Mansel, Treasurer of the Navy under James I, and as dishonest a character as you could ever hope to find. He appears to have taken many hundreds of pounds out of the fund, rarely deposited any money into the Chest, while angrily refusing to present any accounts. An inquiry of 1608 concluded, 'that which should sustain only the poor and impotent and no other,

is perverted … It is lent by those who have no authority and borrowed by those who have no need.[11]

Despite such inquiries, nothing seems to have been done to improve the situation. Indeed, during the year 1617 a second inquiry, again with no resulting improvements, declared,

> Great sums have been collected which should have been put into the chest … and not withstanding that a great part has been charitably and orderly bestowed, yet many other sums of no small amount … have been lent out and do still remain.[12]

Apart from sums of money collected, the Chatham Chest was later financed by rent from certain properties bestowed on the fund by various monarchs. In all cases, such land was situated in North Kent, in close proximity to Chatham, and included Newlands Farm, St Mary Hoo (given to the fund in 1632), Scocles Farm, Minster in Sheppey (1641), Macklands Farm, Rainham (1647), Brook Marsh, Chatham (1636) and the Delce, Rochester (1660). However, embezzlement of the fund continued, with Samuel Pepys, in his famous diaries, referring to another naval treasurer, Sir William Batten, removing fairly large sums. Indeed, during the year 1660 a further enquiry into the affairs of the Chest had to be instigated, but this apparently met on only two occasions, and got little further than the two already mentioned.

11 Chatham Chest, an early pension scheme for seamen, was originally supervised by dockyard officers, with the chest held in the yard. The fund no longer exists, and the chest is now at the National Maritime Museum, Greenwich.

The second of the two charitable institutions established by Sir John Hawkins was the almshouse that still bears his name. Located in the High Street and immediately opposite St Bartholomew's Chapel, it was intended that this should provide support for 'poor mariners or shipwrights who might be maimed or brought into want or poverty'. To this end, the hospital provided houses for a maximum of twelve pensioners, each of whom received in addition a weekly allowance of one shilling. The original buildings were completed in 1592 and were situated around a central courtyard. The pensioners themselves were accommodated in a row of four houses that had their backs to the High Street. Because of this arrangement, entry into the hospital at the time was through Boundary Lane, there being an archway or gate at the top of this road. Further along, there was a second and smaller gate that led directly into the open space or central square of the hospital. Both gates bore inscriptions, the outer archway proclaiming, 'The poor ye shall always have with you to whom you may do good yf ye wyl'; on the inner gate there was a verse from Deuteronomy, part of which declared, 'thou shall open thyne hand unto thy brother'. Both these gateways, together with the original 16th-century buildings, were replaced during the 18th century.

In establishing the almshouse, Hawkins was careful to ensure that it had a sufficient endowment of land to cover future needs. To begin with, the hospital stood on its own freehold, this having been purchased from St Bartholomew's

12 Chatham gained a second major dockyard at the beginning of the 17th century. This was constructed on a site downriver from the Tudor yard on a site now managed by the Chatham Historic Dockyard Trust. Nothing remains of this second yard, most of its buildings, which were of timber, being replaced by brick buildings in the 18th century. This photograph looks across the site of that second dockyard.

Hospital sometime around 1590. Furthermore, a separate area of land had been acquired from the same source but on a 40-year lease. This second piece of land lay on the west side of Boundary Lane, and thus within Rochester, and had upon it various houses including one occupied by the governor of the hospital. The leasehold of this land was regularly renewed (for further periods of 40 years) up until 1792, when it was taken back by the dean and chapter of Rochester. As for the provision of an actual income, the hospital was also provided with further property in Essex. This was Great Garlands Farm in Stanford-le-Hope, its value in the 1590s being £66 per annum.

The growing importance of Chatham is further underlined by the decision, taken at the beginning of the following century, to build a second major dockyard. Constructed just a little further down-river from the original yard, this is the site that is currently managed by the Historic Dockyard Trust. In estimating the cost of moving to the new site, it was felt that £4,000 would be required for construction of the new facilities. To meet such a large financial commitment, it was considered that the government would be well advised to close the dockyard at Deptford, so making a saving of £5,000. Upon completion of the new yard at Chatham, a further saving of £300 would be made, as a number of storehouses being used in Rochester would no longer be required. In the event, neither the dockyard at Deptford nor the storehouses at Rochester were to be relinquished. Instead, the latter formed the basis of a naval victualling yard that remained on

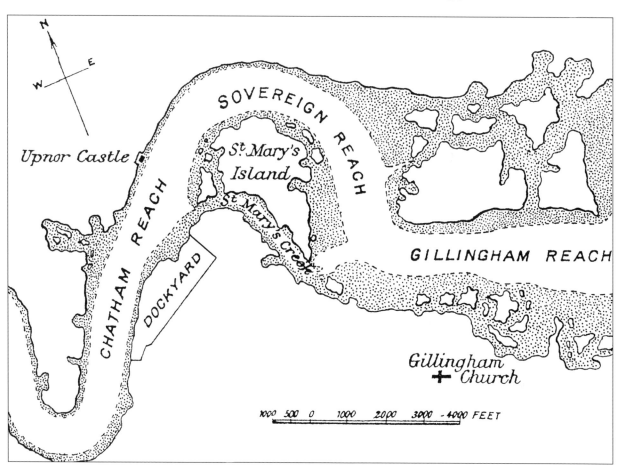

13 The location and original extent of Chatham's second dockyard. Both Chatham and Gillingham Reaches were highly valued stretches of water used both for the mooring and general maintenance of warships. The yard was extended to the east in piecemeal fashion and eventually incorporated St Mary's Island.

the borders of Rochester and Chatham until the early 19th century. As for the dockyard at Deptford, this was retained by the Navy until 1869.

Plans for this second dockyard at Chatham appear to go back to the year 1611, when thought was given to the construction of a dry dock large enough to accommodate three warships. If such a dock were to be built, however, it would also require the construction of suitable workshops, further storehouses and a wharf. Given that the existing dockyard at Chatham covered an area of only 20 acres, a much larger expanse of land would also be required. Thus it became necessary to enter into negotiations with various landowners in the area. Among those with whom the Admiralty had to negotiate was a certain Kenrick Edisbury, Paymaster of the Navy since 1588. Having gained inside knowledge of the government's intentions, he had made a point of buying land on the very site that the government wished to acquire. Purchasing the land from Robert Jackson, who then held the manor, Edisbury made a considerable profit when he sold it to the Admiralty. Despite this example of what is now termed 'insider dealing', Edisbury's contribution was relatively small, the Admiralty gaining the bulk of the land they needed as a result of direct negotiations with Robert Jackson and which led to the following agreement,

> Sir Robert Jackson Kt. for the rent of certaine grounds called Lords Lands containing by estymation 71 acres ... part whereof is used for the newe dockyard and rope waie part for a brick and lyme kiln and part for waies to the Docks and kylns at £14 per annum half a year ended at Christmas 1622 ... £7.[13]

Further parcels of land were acquired from the dean and chapter of Rochester (land formerly owned by St Mary's Church) and West Court Manor.

Construction of the new dry dock, known as a double dock because of its great length and capacity, must have started sometime around 1616. It was completed by 1619, that year also seeing the opening of a mast pond. Additional facilities continued to be added over the following years, and these considerably exceeded the relatively unambitious plans of 1611. In particular, a new wharf was under construction in 1618, its supports made up from three hulked galleons, *Mary Rose* (launched 1556), *Garland* (1590) and *Nuestra Sonora Del Rosario* (captured from Spain in 1588). Regarding this last vessel, the sum of £61 1s. 3d. was paid to

> Thomas Wood, shipwright, and sundry other ... employed in digging out the old Spanish ship at Chatham, near the galley dock, clearing her of all the stubb ballast and other trash within board, making her swim, and removing near unto the mast dock, where she was laid, and sunk for the defence and preservation of the wharf.[14]

As well as the new wharf and a number of new storehouses, the next seven years also saw the erection of a ropehouse (1621), officers' residences (1622) and two more dry docks (1623, 1624). By the time of its completion, the new dockyard at Chatham, which by then was employing in excess of 200 artisans, was undeniably the most important in the country. No other yard, be it Portsmouth, Woolwich or Deptford, could come anywhere near to rivalling the facilities that had now been constructed at Chatham.

Three

A 17th-Century New Town

Then to the Hill House at Chatham where I never was before, and I found a pretty, pleasant house, and am pleased with the arms that hang there.

[From the diary of Samuel Pepys, 8 April 1661]

The use of Chatham Reach as a naval anchorage and the rapid establishment of a major royal dockyard ensured that the nearby village would also witness a massive population increase. At first, however, it was all rather haphazard. In 1575, for instance, 120 shipwrights were brought to the dockyard for the purpose of rapidly repairing and getting to sea a vast number of warships. Their stay at the dockyard was only temporary, all of them returning from whence they came later that same year. Others, though, were more permanently attached to the yard, their numbers soon swamping the three hundred or so who had originally lived in the village. Indeed, by the end of the century, Chatham's population had probably reached about seven hundred.

Some idea of local population growth can be gleaned from the parish registers. From the year 1568 onwards these faithfully record the number of baptisms, marriages and burials taking place at St Mary's Church. While they do not provide an accurate measure of the population, they do indicate the general trend. As proof of this, take the year 1575. The registers clearly reflect the temporary influx of 120 shipwrights, there being a marked increase in the number of recorded marriages and baptisms. Some of those shipwrights may have brought their families with them while others chose to marry locally. The number of marriages for that year rose to eight, almost twice the average for the decade. Similarly, the number of baptisms doubled. However, the most staggering rise was in the number of burials, this reflecting both the dangers of dockyard employment as well as the prevalence of disease in the unhygienic living conditions

Year	Births	Marriages	Burials	Probable cause
1575	14	8	18	Temporary placement of 120 shipwrights
1576	7	3	6	
1577	13	5	5	}Pipe roll accounts show large numbers of additional
1578	7	8	6	}workmen employed on new building works in the yard.
1579	2	5	10	
1580	9	2	7	
1581	9	1	3	Little or no activity in the dockyard and anchorage.
1582	??	2	1	
1583	14	3	5	
1584	12	1	19	
1585	13	4	9	
1586	16	8	19	Fear of Spanish invasion leads to increased naval activity.
1587	13	5	23	Fleet being prepared to meet the threatened Armada.
1588	24	12	32	Final preparations of fleet prior to sailing on 29 April.

Fluctuations in Baptisms, Marriages and Burials at Chatham, 1575-1588[2]

that were forced upon those who came to Chatham. In 1575, the number of those buried at Chatham reached 18 while the average for the decade was only 8.7. Further perusal of these registers shows that other years marked by hectic naval activity also saw a sudden increase in the number of registered baptisms, marriages and burials. Among them was 1588, the year of the Spanish Armada, when a great many ships were brought to the Medway in preparation for the coming conflict. In that year, the number of marriages once again rose to eight while the number of baptisms peaked at 24. However, on this occasion the number of burials reached a staggering 32, reflecting an outbreak of typhus on board warships in the Medway and the subsequent deaths of a number of seamen.[1]

Despite the increasing importance of Chatham, the majority of those who came to the dockyard were not allowed to see it as a permanent place of employment. Instead, they were given temporary lodging allowances which were paid on top of their normal wages. Inevitably, this made Chatham a popular place to work, since those employed here were considerably more affluent than those employed at Woolwich or Deptford where no such allowances were paid. In 1611, for instance, the Christmas quarter witnessed a total of 259 shipwrights, caulkers and other tradesmen receiving lodging money.

It was the continued payment of these allowances that eventually proved a factor in the expansion of the yard at Chatham. In creating that second yard, which would possess all necessary facilities, then it would be possible to sustain a larger permanent work force that was not constantly moving between yards. In the survey of 1611 that directly led to the building of the large double dock at Chatham, it was estimated that an annual saving of £564 could be made if lodging money and other fees were discontinued.

The payment of such allowances did not solve the question of where the increasing numbers arriving in Chatham were supposed to live. As artisans and labourers poured into the village, all available living space quickly disappeared. Later arrivals were forced further afield, often renting rooms in the ale houses and hostelries of Rochester and Gillingham. Not surprisingly, though, the officers of the new yard had a distinct advantage over those they employed. Instead

of having to find accommodation for themselves it was supplied by the Navy. In the new yard, a group of large terraced houses was built specifically for the officers but, even prior to construction of the earlier Tudor yard, the needs of senior officers had been met, the Admiralty renting Hill House for their use. This was a substantial three-storey brick building owned by the dean and chapter of Rochester. Little is known of the early history of the house, although the style in which it was built indicates that it had been constructed only recently. We do know that the Admiralty first acquired the building in 1567, when it was described as a rented house 'wherein the officers of the marine causes doe mete and confere together'. As a result of links with the Navy, which were to continue into the 18th century, the house was known for a time as Queen's House.

Among those who became particularly familiar with Hill House was Phineas Pett. In 1630 he was to become the first resident commissioner of Chatham dockyard, although his associations with Chatham begin a lot earlier. In fact his father, Peter Pett, was a master shipwright at Chatham during the 1580s and was among the first to live at Hill House. Of that period, when still a young boy, Phineas later recalled,

> I was brought up in my father's house at Deptford Strond until I was almost nine years of age, and then put out to a free school at Rochester in Kent, to one Mr Webb, with whom I boarded about one year, and afterwards lay at Chatham Hill in my father's lodging in the Queen's House from whence I went every day to school in Rochester and came home at night for three years space.[3]

Over the following years, Phineas Pett, having completed his shipwright apprenticeship at Chatham, eventually left the town in order to gain experience in other shipyards. Eventually, though, in 1600 he returned to Chatham to take up the post of keeper of the plank yard. As such, he was not of sufficiently senior status to receive accommodation in Hill House; instead, he was forced to use some of his personal wealth to acquire the lease of the manor house.[4] This represents quite an interesting move, for the house was not one that would normally be associated with a mere keeper of the plank yard. In leasing

ÆTAT SVE 43

14 Phineas Pett, a notable long-term resident of 17th-century Chatham. (National Portrait Gallery)

the manor house, Phineas Pett suddenly found himself having to meet an annual rent of £25, at a time when his annual dockyard salary was less than £30. Surely it must have been a result of Chatham's massive housing shortage that led this newly appointed officer to take on such a potentially debt-making burden. That Phineas Pett could afford it, there was no doubt. He came from an extremely wealthy and influential family. Furthermore, he was also aware that he was likely to receive rapid promotion now that he had returned to Chatham. Only two years later, for instance, he was to become assistant master shipwright, with his appointment to master shipwright coming soon after. At this point, he would have been eligible for accommodation at Hill House, but probably remained at the Manor House, it being on a 21-year lease.

For those less well-placed than Phineas Pett, the chance of receiving suitable accommodation was more or less entirely dependent upon land becoming available for the construction of new buildings. At the east end of the village this happened at an an early stage, a number of new houses built along the banks of the Bourne forming a narrow lane that became known as The Brook. Among those who aided the construction of such housing was Phineas Pett himself. Aware that there was considerable money to be made by purchasing suitable building land, Pett decided in 1616 to make a small investment. He noted in his autobiography, 'The 8th day of April, I bought a piece of ground of one Christopher Collier, lying in a place called the Brook at Chatham, for which I paid him £35 ready moneys.'5 Just four weeks later he made a further acquisition, 'The 13th day of May, I bought the rest of the land at the Brook, of John Griffin and Robert Griffin, brothers, and a lease of their sister, belonging to the College of Rochester.'6 A further area of land became available in 1621 when Pett's lease on the manor house came to an end. The owner of the manor, Reginald Barker, who now lived at Boley Hill in Rochester, decided that little would be gained from retaining a house that probably required considerable renovation. Instead, he decided upon its demolition, dividing the demesne land into small plots that were sold to the highest bidders. Finally, a 20-acre area of land called Brookfield became available from about 1650 onwards. Owned by the dean and chapter of Rochester, and sited close to the church, it

was also leased in small plots, some of them of no more than 300 sq. ft.

Upon these various parcels of land, hundreds of new houses were built, their construction often leaving much to be desired. Financed by those who were clearly intent upon making great sums of money, little thought was given to comfort or style. Instead, many of these houses were no more than a single room deep and built in such close proximity to each other that there was little chance of light or air penetrating the interior. In some cases they were built back-to-back, having neither wash house nor toilet. Where this occurred, some twenty or thirty families were forced to share one earth closet which was built in the street outside.

As more and more houses continued to be built, so Chatham was able to claim the distinction of township, albeit as a dirty, unhygienic and overcrowded new town. Not surprisingly, resulting problems were innumerable. Most worrying, for those who lived there, was a continuing rise in the death rate. Examination of the parish registers demonstrates how unhealthy Chatham had become. With a population that would not reach four figures until the mid-century period, the number of deaths was soon averaging in excess of 30 per year. Apart from the persistent presence of smallpox

Burials at Chatham, 1615-1626			
1615	37	1623	40
1616	31	1624	52
1617	30	1625	134
1618	51	1626	68
1619	34	1627	45
1620	32	1628	41
1621	27	1629	25
1622	24	1630	33

and typhus, the overcrowded alleyways encouraged tuberculosis, typhoid and frequent outbreaks of measles. In addition, 1603, 1625 and 1636 were plague years in Chatham, and saw a sudden (and otherwise unaccountable) rise in the number of burials. The year 1603, which also witnessed a severe outbreak of plague in London, saw the number of deaths in Chatham rise to 40, considerably in excess of any other year in this

Numbers dying of the plague between 6 March 1666 and 7 February 1667

March	7	July	135	November	24
April	20	August	111	December	5
May	40	September	75	January	3
June	46	October	66	February	2

decade. However, the most severe of all the plague attacks was the 12-month period between March 1666 and February 1667. During that time, the number of burials in Chatham rocketed to 534. According to an entry in the parish register, 'when the disorders raged at the highest degree, the number of burials amounted to 7, 8 and 9 in the day'.[7]

Undoubtedly, matters might not have been so serious, if Chatham had possessed an administrative body with the necessary authority to prevent the worst aspects of town development. Instead, it had only a vestry, a weak and inefficient body that was overseen by the minister of St Mary's Church. Supposedly, meetings of the vestry were held monthly, with any member of the parish eligible to attend. According to *The Compleat Parish Officer*, a handbook published in 1734,

> A Vestry is the Assembly of the whole Parish, met together for the Dispatch of the Business of the Parish; and this Meeting being commonly held in the Place for keeping the Priest's Vestments, adjoining to or belonging to the Church, it thence has its name of Vestry.[8]

Despite its being very much part of the business of the parish, the vestry had no authority over the planning and layout of the town. Instead, it had to rely upon the good sense and charity of those who were responsible for the building new houses, merely reacting to the problems created by the resulting social conditions.

Among duties specific to the vestry were those of managing the church building, caring for the poor and maintaining the local roads and highways. To this end, members of the Chatham vestry—or at least those who could be bothered to attend—annually elected two churchwardens, two overseers of the poor and a surveyor of the highways. Of these officers, the overseers of the poor were undoubtedly the busiest, responsible

both for the collection of the poor rate and its disbursement to the needy. Providing them with a degree of assistance were the churchwardens, the most superior of the elected officers. They were primarily concerned with the parish church and matters relating to its repair and administration but, since the passing of the Poor Law Act of 1601, they were also supposed to join 'with the overseers of the poor in the execution of their whole office'.[9] The surveyor of the highways carried out a regular inspection of all roads in the area and oversaw any necessary repairs, these being carried out at the expense of the parish: 'Surveyors of the Highways are within four days after the Acceptance of their office and so from Time to Time every four months, to view the Roads, &c, and to present upon oath, such as not in repair ...'[10]

Unfortunately, the surviving minutes belonging to Chatham's 17th-century vestry do not suggest a particularly vibrant or caring community. Indeed, despite a requirement that vestries should meet monthly, the one at Chatham rarely appears to have met more than twice a year. Invariably, the first meeting of the year was not until March, this being the required month for the election of the parish officers. At these meetings, one or two other matters were occasionally dealt with, these invariably of an insignificant nature. At a meeting held on 11 March 1642, when John Rogers, Edward Holborne (churchwardens), James Marsh and Thomas Haddock (overseers) were elected, only one other matter was discussed. This concerned an 11-year-old orphan, Richard Swain, who was threatening to become a burden to the parish. It was agreed that the youngster should be 'entered into a 9 year apprenticeship with Manly Stansill a Gillingham fisherman for the sum of £3'. Stansill agreed 'that Swain will not be a future charge or trouble to the parish of Chatham'. Reading between the lines, it seems clear that the vestry was less concerned with the well being of the unfortunate Richard Swain and more concerned that he should not be a future burden upon those who paid the Chatham poor rate.

The middle years of the century proved a particularly difficult time for the vestry as it had to meet head-on the massive political and religious changes that the country was then witnessing. In 1643, with the nation in the midst of civil war, those who controlled the vestry were clearly in sympathy with the Parliamentary cause. In June of that year, it was determined that the communion table should be removed to the body of the church, this being in accord with Puritan philosophy. Later in that year, £12 13s. was collected for the support of Parliamentarian soldiers wounded at the Battle of Edgehill.[11]

Those who opposed the king at Chatham did not have it all their own way, however. In 1648, a number of those living in the town gave their support to a large-scale royalist uprising that attempted to seize both the dockyard and ships moored in the Medway. Only the valiant efforts of the dockyard commissioner, Peter Pett, son of Phineas, prevented the scheme achieving complete success. For those of the vestry who supported Parliament, a much greater danger came in 1660 with the restoration of the monarchy. This resulted in a certain amount of political purging, some of those on the vestry trying to conceal their earlier activities. Doubtless, this explains why a number of pages from the vestry minute book have been removed. However, this desperate act was insufficient to save Walter Rosewell, the curate of the parish. Having been appointed by Parliament in 1647, he was quickly removed from office in 1661.

As for the activities of the vestry during those unrecorded years, a small clue is to be found in the parish registers of the period. Here it is recorded that the vestry was failing to carry out one of its most basic duties, that of overseeing the work of its elected officers. In 1653, it eventually came to light that the parish clerk was failing to record the names of those who were baptised and buried at St Mary's Church. To rectify this, a special meeting was held on 22 November 1653 in which the clerk, John Beckett, was severely censured. Furthermore, it was decided that a new register should be opened, with Beckett ordered to enter into this book

'the names of every such person and persons on the register within six daies who have been buried since the 27th September last'.[12]

The failings of the vestry in Chatham contrast sharply with the administration of neighbouring Rochester. Since the incorporation of the city in 1464, a mayor (then known as a bailiff) together with a deputy was selected from among the burgesses of the city. Once in office, the mayor had the sole right to pass various bye-laws, although it is assumed he had an advisory council. These laws, which had to be for the benefit of the city, were enforceable through the existence of various courts: the 'pie powder' court, justice court and latterly quarter sessions. These rights were confirmed during the 17th century when a new charter of August 1629 permitted the formation of a common council that was to consist of the mayor, annually elected, together with 11 aldermen and 12 assistants. With the exception of the mayor, each was to hold office for the period of 'their natural lives'. Upon the death of any member, the remainder were to select a successor. Although the common council was a self-perpetuating oligarchy that would often abuse its own powers, it did have the necessary authority to regulate the kind of developments that, in Chatham, were wreaking havoc. The charter of 1629, for instance, specifically gave the common council the right to pass 'such reasonable Laws, Statutes and Ordnances' as were necessary 'for the good ruling and government of the citizens'. As such, it not only passed laws that controlled housing development, the disposal of refuse and commercial transactions, but it had in its possession much larger sums of money to be used for the purpose of ameliorating problems and difficulties. By meeting in the Guildhall, an early civic building that dominated the lower High Street, the Common Council also possessed a highly visible symbol of its authority which contrasts with the lowly vestry room from where Chatham was ineffectually administered.

The town of Chatham, through its lack of such an influential body, was also disadvantaged in its dealings with such a powerful neighbour. The town's sudden growth was not looked upon with much favour by those who lived in Rochester. The influential businessmen of the Common Council clearly saw it as a threat. To this end, efforts were occasionally made to curtail the economic progress of their less than attractive rival. One battle ensued over the right of Chatham to hold both a fair and market, these seen as being in direct competition with those that Rochester had long possessed. The market at Chatham was first set up in the dockyard sometime prior to 1666 and was designed to allow the yard workforce to buy food without going into town. This was later extended into a Saturday market and fair, now situated in the vicinity of Fair Row (obliterated by the Pentagon in the 1970s). Such developments were deemed by the Corporation as being in contravention of their own charter and they resorted to legal proceedings which brought a temporary cessation to the Chatham market. Fortunately, the expanding township had one very powerful ally in the form of the Admiralty. The whole matter was brought to their attention in April 1674, the minutes of the Board recording,

> Mr Speaker informing my Lords of the design now on foot by the Town of Rochester in the renewal of their Charter to bring the town of Chatham within their jurisdiction. It was referred to the Officers of the Navy to consider and give their Lordships their advice concerning the same.[13]

Following this, the Admiralty advised Parliament of their opposition to this move, so bringing an end to Rochester's rather spurious objections.

Chatham had one thing going for it. Levels of poverty were much lower than those found in other Kentish towns. The rate books of the period, which indicate both those who paid the poor rate as well as those who were too poor to pay, show that about seventy per cent of the population were expected to meet the demands of the parish overseer. In other Kentish towns, notably Maidstone and Tonbridge, the numbers deemed unable to pay were usually in the region of fifty per cent. That Chatham should appear so affluent was a direct result of the dockyard and the long-term job security it provided. Many of those who lived in other towns were reliant upon seasonal or occasional employment, while those at the dockyard were employed throughout the year. Dockyard wage levels were also fairly high and certainly provided artisans with a relatively comfortable lifestyle. At the top of the wage structure were the shipwrights and caulkers, both paid at the rate of 2s. 1d. per day, while other well-paid workers were joiners, house carpenters and sailmakers, who were all paid between 1s. 8d. and 1s. 10d. per day. At the lower end of the scale were labourers, who received 1s. 1d. per day. These were the rates laid down in the 1690s, although amounts prior to that decade would not have been greatly different as levels of inflation were insignificant, and wages remained static for most of the century.

Outside the dockyard there was by now a wide range of alternative employers as well as other artisans who chose self-employment. It was necessary for such people to receive an income that was at least comparable with the dockyard; if anything, it had to be slightly higher in order to make up for the more seasonal or temporary nature of such work. For this reason, the churchwardens at Chatham had to pay above average rates when they required alterations to be made to St Mary's Church in May 1636. John Davies, a carpenter, was paid at the rate of 2s. 4d. per day, while his assistant received 1s. 6d. per day. In addition, two labourers were paid at the daily rate of 1s. 3d. 'to lay up the shingle'. Shortly afterwards, the churchwardens were paying the bricklayers at the rate of 2s. 4d.

Some were paid a fixed rate for completion of a certain task. Henry Cony, a brick and lime burner at Chatham, seems to have struck a highly lucrative arrangement with Captain Osborne of Hartlip. The arrangement was that 88,000 bricks should be supplied at the rate of 5s. per thousand. In addition, Cony was also allowed £3 to prepare his kilns. It is likely that, with all the house building and frequent new construction work in the dockyard, Cony not only employed others, but had a guarantee of frequent work as a result of all those demands. As such, he was probably an extremely wealthy artisan.

For those who worked at the dockyard, the biggest single issue was not so much wage rates as the infrequency of their payment. In 1626, some 300 shipwrights, artificers and labourers employed in the yard petitioned for an immediate payment of wages. In the 12 months preceding this petition, they had not received a single penny, many of them being forced to pawn furniture and clothing to survive. Matters were no better in 1648, when recourse to a petition had once again become necessary:

Amongst other crying necessities we make bold to represent to the Honorable Commissioners ye sad and indigent condition of the ordinary here which besides the want of their wages for near these 2 years are for these 3 weeks past deprived of Victualls from Mr. Robinson, by means whereof having already spent what they had in maintenance of themselves and families, they are now driven to that extremity that some go about the county to seek for work, others to beg or borrow.[14]

The lateness in payment of wages continued to be a major problem for those employed in the dockyard for much of the rest of the century and it was a point frequently remarked upon by Samuel Pepys in his diaries. Pepys is actually an excellent commentator on events in the dockyard, serving as Clerk of the Acts on the Navy Board from 1660 to 1673. This was the body that governed the yards, but it was not technically responsible for late payment of wages. That was something that had to be placed squarely on

a series of governments that had run the nation into debt, using dockyard wages to fund other pressing commitments. By Pepys' time, the Navy had entered into debts amounting to £1 million, resulting in the yard workers at Chatham both drawing up petitions and marching on London. Even injured and ailing seamen, those reliant upon the Chatham Chest, were affected. According to Pepys, in a letter to Sir William Coventry, a fellow Navy Commissioner:

> I have every week complaints from the governors that for want of money they have not received a penny since December 1663 and poor wretches for relief forced to come crawling up hither that would break one's heart to see them.[15]

On the whole, however, the dockyard wage (when paid) was fairly generous and only occasionally, led to complaints. One group that did feel dissatisfaction were the ropemakers and spinners. By 1675 the spinners of Chatham dockyard were in receipt of 1s. 10d. for a day's

15 Samuel Pepys, Clerk of the Acts to the Navy Board, was a frequent visitor to Chatham. There are numerous references to the town and its dockyard in his diaries.

16 In 1675, the spinners and ropemakers of Chatham dockyard took strike action upon the introduction of new work regulations. This mannequin ropeyard spinner is among the exhibits to be seen within the present-day ropery overseen by the Chatham Historic Dockyard Trust.

work but were incensed by an order given in May of that year ordering them to spin a minimum of 18 threads of yarn instead of the previous seventeen. On 25 May, John Owen, the clerk of the ropeyard at Chatham, informed his superiors in London, 'This daie all the workmen imployed in his Majesty's Ropeyard here, refused to do the stint, which I am commanded to see performed by the late instructions received from yr hands'.[16] As a partial solution, Owen refused to register as present any of the ropeyard workers. In doing so he was not barring their entry into the ropeyard, for he further informed those at the Navy Board that he intended to make a separate note of the names of those who did enter, together with any 'works performed by them'.

The situation at the ropery was allowed to ride until the beginning of July. Those coming into work were permitted to carry out any tasks they could undertake, but no payments were to be made. On 1 July, Owen wrote again to the Board. He pointed out that he was unable to make up the Quarter Books until a decision was taken as to the future of those workers standing out and the amounts to be paid to those still working. On receipt of this letter, the Board decided to adopt a much tougher stance. It was decided that all those ropemakers at Chatham who refused to work according to the new instructions were to be immediately dismissed.

Knowing that they could not possibly win, the Chatham ropemakers chose only to stand out for a further five days. Prompting the final return was a promise that if work were resumed within the next two or three 'daies', then any man agreeing to the new rules would be re-instated. According to John Owen:

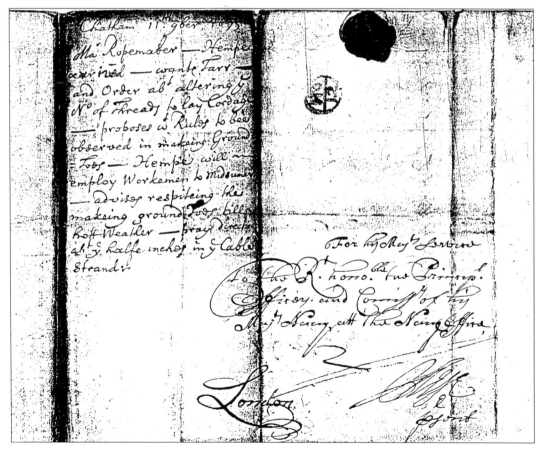

17 The letter of which this is only the first page is from the Clerk of the Rope Yard at Chatham and requests further information as to the new conditions of work. (Public Record Office ADM 106/309, f198)

18 A model of *Prince*, a warship launched at Chatham dockyard in 1670. The immense amount of rope that went into the rigging of such a warship can be seen clearly. All of the rope for this vessel would have been manufactured within the dockyard.

These are to acquaint your honors the 13 Instant in the morning, all the ropemakers made their appearance in the ropeground, and every man answered to his name, being willing to work according to the late Rules … [17]

Before concluding this study of 17th-century Chatham, a brief reference needs to be made to one other important event, the Dutch raid of 1667. In that year, a squadron of Dutch warships sailed into the Medway and attempted to destroy the dockyard. There must have been a

19 Spinners at work in the dockyard ropery. This collection of views demonstrates how hemp was first spun into yarn and then warped into strands.

considerable fear that, had the Dutch been successful in this task, they might also have wreaked havoc upon the town itself. In the event, they got no further than Upnor Castle. Many of those who lived in Chatham were either witness to the passing events or were themselves involved. Among them was the dockyard commissioner, Peter Pett, whom Pepys recorded in his diary as being 'in a very fearful stink for fear of the Dutch, and desires help for God and the King and kingdom's sake'.[18] Another Chatham resident, Thomas Wilson, the Navy victualler, together with his assistant, Mr. Gordon, provided members of the Navy Board with a first-hand account of the progress of the Dutch squadron. Somewhere off Gillingham they had seen 'three ships burnt, they lying all dry, and boats going from the men-of-war to fire them'. The two men also reported hearing English voices upon the Dutch ship, these were seamen who did 'cry

and say, "We did heretofore fight for tickets; now we fight for Dollars!" '. In other words, these were English seamen who had joined the Dutch because they were no longer prepared to fight for promissory notes (or tickets) but preferred actual cash in hand, in the form of Dutch 'Dollars'.[19]

It was this same late payment of wages that was causing concern among the dockyard workers of Chatham. They, too, rejected government promises of future payment and chose to withdraw their services during the period of crisis. Most seemed to take the view that, if the government would not pay them, then there was little reason why they should risk their lives. According to the Duke of Albemarle, who commanded the English fleet in the Medway, 'I found scarce twelve of eight hundred men which were then in the King's pay, in His Majesty's yard, and these so

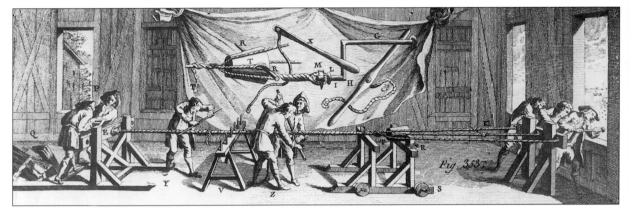

distracted with fear that I could have little or
no service from them'.

Once the Dutch retreated, the yard men
began to return, but even then they were reluctant
to work without wages. To encourage them, they
were offered a shilling a day extra. According to
William Brouncker, a Navy commissioner, this
failed to enthuse them:

> But all this stops not the mouths of the yard,
> who have two quarters [six months' pay]
> due to them, and say they deserted not the
> service but for mere want of bread, not
> being able to live without their pay. We are
> fain to give them good words, but doubt
> whether that will persuade them to stand in
> the day of trial.[20]

Despite the importance of the Dutch raid for
British history, little more needs to be added
here.[21] Its influence on the town of Chatham was
peripheral, if only because the Dutch failed to
achieve their ultimate objective. Instead, most of
the fighting took place off Gillingham. On the
other hand, the raid does demonstrate the importance of the dockyard at Chatham. At that time,
it was the largest naval yard in the country, with
the Dutch determined upon its destruction for
this very reason. Employing, as it did, hundreds
of skilled artisans, the dockyard was now the life-
blood of Chatham and the reason for its continued
existence as a town.

20 The final process of ropemaking involved laying
strands on the ropehouse floor for conversion into rope.

21 An interesting contrast with the method used for
manufacturing rope in the 17th and 18th centuries is
provided by this present-day view. It shows the machinery
used in the modern dockyard ropery. Although it is fairly
old, it is still of a sophistication that was undreamed of
some three hundred years ago.

Four

An Industrial-Military Complex

Chatham Dockyard is situated on the Medway near to Rochester, 10 leagues distant from London and six leagues from the sea. There are in this Dockyard two building slips for building ships of war and five dry docks for repairing and graving.

'Remarks on the English Navy', Blaise Ollivier (1737)

By the beginning of the 18th century, Chatham had become a place of considerable importance within the nation's rapidly growing military machine. Apart from its massive and still expanding dockyard, the town possessed two further military installations: a victualling yard and a gun wharf. While the former supplied all the food needs of warships entering and leaving the Medway, the latter was responsible for the storage of guns and other shipboard weapons. Both the victualling yard and ordnance wharf were large-scale employers of civilian labour and, together with the dockyard, helped ensure that Chatham was totally dependent upon the war machine for its prosperity and future progress.

In particular, the dockyard had seen many thousands of pounds spent on it, and the work force had reached a figure now in excess of one thousand. Among the more notable additions to the yard during these years were two further dry docks (completed in 1685), a brick storehouse for the ropery (1686), ten mast houses and a second mast pond (1686), a new house for the commissioner of the yard (1703), terraced housing for the officers (1722-31) and completion of the dockyard wall and gateway (1720). All these were very significant structures and continued to ensure that the dockyard was the largest employer of industrial labour in the south east. Celia Fiennes, who visited Chatham in 1697, was particularly impressed by the nature of the work carried out,

> I saw severall large shipps building others refitting; there was in one place a sort of arches like a bridge of brick-work, they told me the use of it was to let in the water there and so they put their masts into season ... [1]

Another who provides a description of the yard is Daniel Defoe. He wrote this account sometime in the 1720s,

> This being the chief arsenal of the Royal Navy of Great Britain. The buildings here are indeed like the ships themselves, surprisingly large, and in their several kinds beautiful. The ware-houses, or rather streets of warehouses, and store-houses for laying up the naval treasures are the largest in dimension, and the most in number that are to be seen anywhere in the world.[2]

The victualling yard grew out of the numerous storehouses that appear to have lined

22 A number of important improvements were made to the dockyard during the early part of the 18th century. Among them was the construction of a house for the Resident Commissioner. It appears that George St Loe, on appointment as commissioner to the yard, was unhappy with the existing accommodation and insisted that a completely new building should be erected for his use.

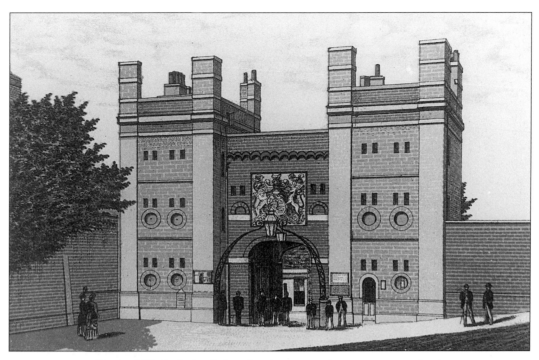

23 In 1720, both the dockyard and present main gate were completed.

24 Apart from the Resident Commissioner, the yard officers themselves were also given new accommodation. This consisted of a terrace of 12 grand houses that differed slightly in size and style to reflect the status of the various officers. The impressive nature of these houses extended even to the elaborate porch depicted in this photograph.

the Medway during the 16th century. While many of these stores contained items necessary for the repair of ships, others must have contained vast quantities of victuals that would have been necessary for those who manned these ships. Eventually, a properly constituted victualling yard was established at the west end of the High Street, some of the storehouses straddling the border into Rochester. As the importance of the anchorage continued to increase, so did the size of the victualling yard, which began to develop its resources and eventually acquired pickling, baking, cutting and slaughterhouses, together with a cooperage. Further expansion occurred at the turn of the century. In 1695, land leased from St Batholomew's Hospital was used for the establishment of an office while additional storehouses were acquired in the following decade. Even so, the needs of the victualling yard were far from satisfied. In 1741, the Victualling Board felt constrained to write to the Admiralty pointing out that there was then an urgent need for a new purpose-built storehouse:

> The great inconvenience We find daily from want of sufficient Store Room at the Port of Chatham renders it necessary to enclose you

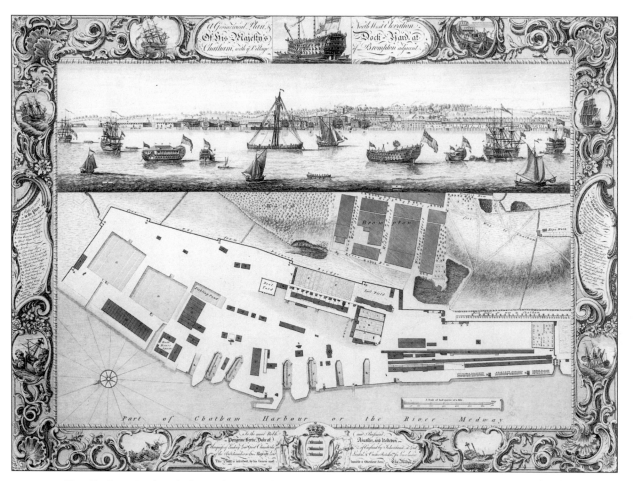

25 Chatham Dockyard, from Thomas Milton's engraving of 1755. The extent of the dockyard and its facilities may be readily appreciated. By that year, the dockyard, including the ropery, had a work force in excess of 1,700.

herewith, we sometime since caused to be made, of the expense of erecting a proper building for the more Commodious carrying on the service there the amount whereof is four hundred and eighteen pounds eight shillings and ninepence farthing, We pray you to lay the same before the Right Honorable Lord Commissioners of the Admiralty for our receiving the necessary Directions, in case the doing thereof meets with their Lordships approval … [3]

Unlike the dock and victualling yards, the ordnance wharf was not a naval establishment. Instead it was administered by the War Office through the Ordnance Board. This was an unusual arrangement, as it meant that the Navy had no direct responsibility for its own guns. Instead,

it had to rely upon a branch of the Army for the manufacture, upkeep and storage of all shipboard ordnance.

The Chatham gun wharf was established in the early part of the 16th century and now stood on the site of the original Tudor dockyard. This arrangement had come about in 1666, when the Navy Board had finally decided to abandon the earlier site, locating all its resources within the area of the later yard. At some point the original dry dock was filled in, while the Ordnance Board was able to make good use of the former dock-yard storehouses. At first, this area continued to be referred to as 'the old dock', but gradually the term gun wharf was introduced. The Ordnance Board began to plan out the area, making it more suitable for their particular needs. The older

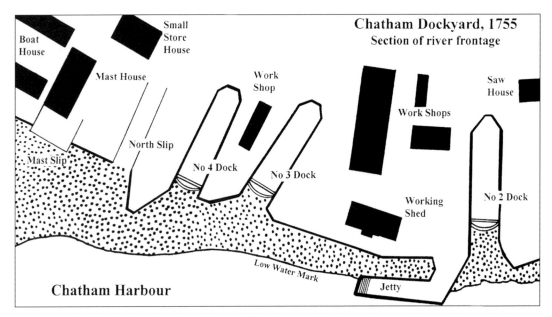

26 Detail of the dockyard based on Thomas Milton's map. This shows the central area of the yard, where ships were built and repaired.

derelict buildings were replaced, while in 1708 a new long storehouse was erected. Over the next 30 years, further carriage sheds, cranes and a master gunner's house were added.

As regards essential usage, the gun wharf was to change very little, and a description by Edward Hasted from the 1770s could apply to the beginning as well as to the end of the century:

> The guns belonging to the royal shipping in this river are deposited on this wharf in long tiers, and large pyramids of canon-balls are

laid up on it, ready for service; there is likewise a continued range of storehouses, in which is deposited the carriage of the guns, and every other kind of store, usually under the care of this office; in one of them is a small armoury of muskets, pistols, cutlasses and pikes, poleaxes, and other hostile weapons arranged in proper order. This department of the ordnance is under the management of a storekeeper, who has a good house here to reside in, a clerk of the survey and a clerk of the cheque … [4]

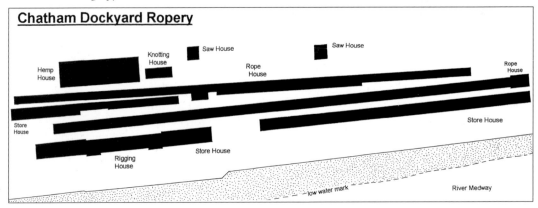

27 Detail of the ropery, based on Milton's map. Most of the buildings at this time were of timber construction, having been built during 1620. Administered separately from the rest of the dockyard, the ropeyard work force in 1755 accounted for 160 artisans and labourers.

To this can be added Brayley's description of 1808:

> The Ordnance Wharf which is not unfrequently called the Old Dock occupies a narrow slip of land below the chalk cliff, between the Church and the river. Here, great quantities of naval ordnance are deposited in regular tiers, and abundance of canon-balls piled up in large pyramids. Great numbers of gun carriages are also laid up under cover; and in the Store houses, and small Armoury, are vast quantities of offensive weapons, as pistols, cutlasses, pikes, pole-axes &tc.[5]

The problem for any town completely dominated by one industrial enterprise is that the prosperity of all those who live there is entirely dependent upon the fortunes of that one industry. For the newly emergent town of Chatham, the good times were associated with the nation's need for a large fleet. Any period of war, or national emergency, was generally good news, while the threat of peace was likely to be accompanied by some form of economic decline. As such, the late 17th century could not have proved better. Although the Anglo-Dutch wars were concluded by the Treaty of Westminster in 1674, this had quickly been followed by a bout of wars with France. The first of these, King William's War, broke out in 1689 and lasted for eight years. Additional periods of hostility took place in the new century, the War of Spanish Succession (1702-1713) quickly followed by the Jacobite

28 In 1755, the Master Ropemaker at Chatham was William Guy, who had succeeded his father, George Guy, in the office. Their joint memorial is found in St Mary's Church.

29 A typical 18th-century dockyard scene depicted by a model. To the left a ship has been hauled down for the cleaning of its hull, while to the right a newly-built ship awaits its superstructure. The cranes and timber store sheds (situated to the rear) were typical of those found at Chatham dockyard. (Science Museum)

30 Chatham dockyard timber storehouses, constructed in the 1770s. Compare these with the model on the previous page.

31 A 19th-century view of the gun wharf. This was another large-scale local employer which added to Chatham's increasing military importance.

32 One of the most notable survivors from the 18th-century gun wharf is the *Command House* pub. The building once served as the house of the Deputy Armament Supply Officer.

33 Further surviving evidence for the existence of the gunwharf is the wall that once surrounded this important military site.

34 Although responsibility for the care of the poor was of the parish's, additional help was frequently provided by sizeable monetary bequests by local notables. This memorial in St Mary's Church relates to such a bequest, given by Sir Edward Gregory, a one-time dockyard Resident Commissioner.

uprisings (1715-19). At that point, however, Chatham hit a serious problem. The year 1719 saw the successful defeat of an attempted Spanish invasion in support of the Jacobites, and the country was suddenly thrust into a long-term period of peace. Large numbers of warships were recalled from around the waters of Europe and simply moored in the Medway until such time as they would once again be fitted out for sea service. Those employed in the dockyard, victualling yard and gun wharf found they had little to do. Numbers employed were drastically reduced, while those still in employment lost their once profitable overtime. In the dockyard, where numbers employed had peaked at 1,175 in 1719, employment in 1725 had fallen to 763.[6] Similarly, in the victualling yard, where 64 artisans and labourers were employed in 1713, only 53 were working by 1717.[7] Chatham had entered into a 20-year period of decline, broken only by the occasional order for the construction of a new warship and the need to survey and keep in repair the fifty or more ships that were now permanently moored in the Medway.

It was the officers of the parish vestry who were the first to register the full impact of this sudden reversal in the town's fortunes. As already demonstrated, the Chatham vestry was a fairly ineffectual body, but it was empowered with a degree of legal authority and was expected to attend to the needs of the poor. Undertaking this work without payment (or any form of training), the degree of commitment would vary from year to year. At first, the task might not have been too irksome. After all, the demands of the Navy ensured that most of those living within the parish could be certain of finding some sort of employment and therefore did not need the help of the parish. With the sudden crisis that fell on Chatham during the 1720s, the demands on the overseers increased four-fold. Whereas in 1684 the total sum of money collected and paid out to the poor was £198 13s. 6d., this sum had increased to nearly £900 by 1724.

As the crisis deepened, it no longer seemed possible to meet the needs of the poor by traditional means. In the past, those seeking the help of the parish might be offered a weekly cash sum or accommodation in one of a number of houses leased by the vestry. The demands of the poor having greatly increased, and the numbers able to pay the poor rate having decreased, it was decided

that an alternative was required. At a meeting of the vestry held at the beginning of 1724, it was resolved that a parish workhouse should be built. Within this building would be housed all of those claiming relief, irrespective of whether they had previously been housed at the expense of the parish or were in receipt of cash payments. Once brought into the workhouse, and assuming they were physically capable, all would be expected to undertake various tasks that would help meet the cost of their upkeep.

To oversee construction of this new building, a special committee was formed from among those who attended vestry meetings. Membership of this committee was somewhat exclusive, consisting only of those who were affluent enough to subscribe substantial sums of money towards the cost of constructing the new poor house. From then on, these and only these individuals had a say in the location, design and future running of the work house. However, not all of those individuals were involved in the day-to-day affairs of the future workhouse, a smaller working committee being elected from among their number:

> At the vestry held in the Parish Church of Chatham in the County of Kent on the 21st day of October 1724 by such of the Parishioners as had subscribed to building a Workhouse for employing the Poor of the said Parish and have nominated and chosen from amongst themselves the seven following persons for managing and carrying forward to purchase land and building to be erected thereon viz. The Honble Tho Kempthorne Esq, Tho Best, Wm Walter, Andw Hawes, Mr Cha Finch, Mr Benj Rosewell and Jos Dodd.[8]

At this same gathering, the subscribers also agreed

> to pay in their severall & respective Subscriptions between the 31st of this Instant & Lady Day of the 25th of March 1725, and that Mr. John Proby and Mr. John Austen do and shall collect Moneys subscribed by the sd Parishioners and shall receive all which moneys as soon as collected shall be paid into the hands of Mr. William Walter who is chosen and appointed treasurer for receiving and paying away the Same According to the directions of any four or more of the above Trustees for the use of the sd parish workhouse … [9]

35 This memorial is to Sir Edward Gregory, who was appointed resident commissioner in 1689 and continued to hold office until 1703. According to the information on this plaque, Sir Edward died on 16 September 1713, having achieved 74 years.

It seems clear that the land upon which the workhouse was to be constructed had already been identified by the date of this important meeting. It was at the east end of the High Street at a point where space still existed for the construction of new buildings. Nevertheless, it was still necessary to demolish a few existing properties, of which one was a house leased by a certain Commander Davies. As compensation for his eviction, he was allowed 'three pounds ten shillings out of the Parish Stock'.[10]

Construction of the workhouse began at the beginning of 1725 and was completed in 1727. Shortly after building work had commenced, it

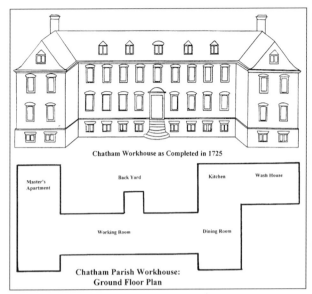

Chatham Workhouse as Completed in 1725

| Master's Apartment | Back Yard | | Kitchen | Wash House |

| Working Room | | Dining Room | |

Chatham Parish Workhouse: Ground Floor Plan

36 Chatham Workhouse as completed in 1725.

was realised that the subscriptions raised would be unable to meet the cost of furnishing the house. At a vestry meeting held on 8 March 1725, further thought was given to the financing of this massive project, and agreement reached to raise a loan 'to buy goods proper and necessary for furnishing the sd house'. The churchwardens were instructed

> to borrow and receive of any Person or Persons who will advance and lend the same any sum or sums of money (not exceeding the whole of the Sum of One Hundred Pounds) to be paid back in one year.[11]

Completed in 1727, the workhouse was a massive three-storey brick building that dominated the local skyline. Built around an extensive courtyard, the upper floor, together with an additional attic storey, provided sleeping accommodation for most of the prospective inmates, with separate areas for orphaned children, the able-bodied poor, unmarried mothers and the aged. None were entitled to a bed, but given only a mattress of sacking that was filled with straw. Least fortunate were the sick and insane. They were relegated to the cellar, an area that not only suffered from dampness but had a constantly leaking and heavily used privy. The ground floor was a communal area that housed the kitchen, dining hall and wash house. A huge work room was also located on this floor and used for a variety of tasks that included oakum picking, sewing and spinning of cloth.

Unfortunately, despite the hopes of those responsible for its construction, the new workhouse did not solve the problems of Chatham's needy. During the years in which it had been under construction, the crisis caused by the long period of peace had simply deepened. The numbers calling upon the overseers for support soon to exceed the numbers for which the workhouse had been planned. As a result, there was serious overcrowding which resulted in a number of inmates having to sleep on the floor.

There were several charities within the parish that also attempted to alleviate the suffering of the poor. Among them were the two late 16th-century charities, the Chatham Chest and Sir John Hawkins' Hospital. The former was now in a much healthier state than it had been in earlier years. Those responsible for managing the Chest were far more thorough in their duties, and several additional sources of income had been acquired. Apart from the farm lands already listed, James II had recently allocated to the Chest part of the money levied on all foreign ships using British ports. According to his instructions, this money was to be used for 'the relief of wounded and decayed Seamen, their Widows and Children'.

The Sir John Hawkins' Hospital was also in a more affluent state, having been the frequent recipient of a number of bequests. Among the more remarkable of these was £60 left by an able seaman who died on board *Hampton Court* during the Battle of La Hogue. To commemorate the gift of such a large sum from a person serving on the lower decks, the Governors of the Hospital chose to have a memorial stone erected and which contained the following inscription:

> In gratitude to the memory of Robert Davis, an honest and able seaman, slain in battle the 19th May 1692. Who by will left Dame Elizabeth Narborough (now Shovell) his sole executrix and the charitable dispenser of his effects the whole amounting to seventy-six pounds and four shillings. Sixty pound whereof was by that worthy lady allotted and paid towards the relief of this decaying foundation. In due acknowledgment of which this stone and inscription were, by order of the Governors of the Hospital, fixed here Anno 1706.[12]

Neither of these two charities was specifically for the needs of those living in Chatham, although many of the seamen and dockyard workers from the town would have received support from one or other of them. On the other hand, the sum of £100 bequeathed to the vestry by Sir Edward Gregory was intended only for the benefit of the 'necessitous' poor who lived within the parish. The Gregorys were a long established Chatham family, Sir Edward serving the dockyard in the capacity of Clerk of the Cheque (1665-89) and resident Commissioner (1689-1703). Upon his death in 1713, the monetary bequest was initially placed in South Seas capital stock and left there until 1720, when it was profitably sold for £750. This fortuitous increase in the value of the bequest allowed for the purchase of the 32-acre Potts Farm that lay within the parish of Burham. In leasing this estate, the vestry secured a regular annual income of £25, which money was used in support of the poor at Chatham. A second charitable bequest for the poor of Chatham was made by Thomas Manley upon his death in 1687. It came in the form of a 10-shilling annual charge upon his farm at Waldeslade, the money to be used for distributing bread to poor widows attending divine service.

Chatham town was also affected by the period of wholesale unemployment that followed upon the restoration of peace in 1719. Whereas the preceding four decades had witnessed a considerable increase in the numbers living in the town, the reverse was now taking place. Many of the artisans, together with their families, who had come to Chatham in search of employment, were now leaving to seek their fortunes elsewhere. Evidence for this comes from a combination of sources, of which the poor rate returns and parish registers are most useful.

The poor rate returns were produced each year and listed all households in the parish. They were used by the collector of poor rates and against each household was marked the amount each had been assessed to pay. In fact, the returns have an additional value as they also show the number of households who were considered unable to pay the poor rate because of their own limited income. These assessments show that, during the year 1684, Chatham had a total of 428 rated properties. It is also possible to arrive at a figure for the town's population at this point in time, by multiplying the number of households by the figure of five.

This particular multiplier has been chosen as it closely reflects the house/person density revealed by the first official government census of 1801. The census actually reveals that in Chatham the number of persons per household was nearer 5.5, but this particular figure may be too high as the census coincided with a massive and recent population boom when housing could not possibly have kept pace with demand. The use of five as a multiplier is still contentious and other historians, looking at other towns, have used a still lower figure.[13] But any number lower than five would be unrealistic as it would fail to reflect the high number of multi-occupational households that characterised Chatham throughout this period of expansion.

Taking the multiplier of five, then, the population of Chatham in the year 1684 would have stood at approximately 2,100. Using the hearth tax as a basis for measuring growth, Chatham's population appears to have been at a slightly higher level in 1665. As with the poor rate, this was a tax upon all wealthier householders, those in receipt of poor relief or occupying houses worth less than 20 shillings excluded from paying the tax. For Chatham, the hearth tax return for 1665 reveals a total of 434 houses.[14] Again, using a multiplier of five, this would suggest a population of about 2,170. Outwardly, this might suggest a period of stagnation; in fact, quite the opposite was taking place. Apart from a single 12-month period, these years probably witnessed a period of continual growth. However, that exception, March 1666 to February 1667, were the months in which Chatham witnessed the calamity of the plague, when the population of the town fell by 25 per cent, reducing the total to approximately 1,600. By 1684, the town was witnessing such a high growth rate that it had almost completely recovered from that earlier demographic disaster.

The poor rate returns also show that the period 1684 to 1720 witnessed a further and quite dramatic increase in the population. By 1720 there were over 1,100 properties assessed in Chatham, indicating a population of 5000.[15] However, because of the onset of peace and the resulting high unemployment, Chatham suffered a further, if less dramatic, demographic disaster, with a steady trickle of artisan families choosing to desert the town. This is best revealed by the baptismal records. In the first 10 years of the new century,

the number of baptisms celebrated at St Mary's Church averaged 200 a year. By the 1720s, this had fallen to 193.[16] In other words, the young and able-bodied, the ones most likely to have children, were now leaving the town.

Upon the outbreak of the prosaically named War of Jenkins' Ear in 1739, Chatham's military complex began to seek out and recruit a much enlarged workforce. The dockyard in 1738 had a workforce of 1,300, but this number had risen to a new high of 1,700 by 1742.[17] Furthermore, these new arrivals to Chatham were beginning to put down roots, and both they and their descendants were to remain in the town for several generations. This is again borne out by the baptismal records of St Mary's Church, which show that in the five-year period following the outbreak of war, the average number of baptisms stood at 212.[18] The probability that these new arrivals remained for several generations—and that many of their descendants may still remain in the Chatham area—is increased by the demands that were placed on the Chatham military complex for the remainder of the century. Following the period of peace, the nation entered into a series of wars that continued until 1815. As the War of Jenkins' Ear became absorbed into the wider struggle of the War of the Austrian Succession, this period of hostility did not end until 1748. Only eight years later, in 1756, the Seven Years War broke out (1756-1763), and this was followed by the American Revolutionary War (1775-1783), the French Revolutionary War (1793-1801) and the Napoleonic Wars (1803-1815). As a result, the dockyard and other military establishments were rarely given the opportunity to run down the work force. Even in the midst of a period of peace, such as the years 1773 or 1785, the numbers employed in the dockyard did not fall below 1,600.[19] Furthermore, during the peak of the wartime periods, the yard boosted its work force to a number that eventually exceeded 2,000.[20] As a result, those who entered dockyard service during the mid-century period rarely found their job security threatened and would have had little or no reason to seek employment outside Chatham.

Of equal importance to Chatham as a naval and military complex was the decision to provide a massive defensive line to defend both the dockyard and ordnance wharf from a landward attack.

37 Chatham barracks, since renamed Kitchener barracks, was originally completed in 1760. In subsequent years it was to be extensively enlarged.

Consisting of earthwork bastions with ditches and ramparts, the scheme was first projected towards the beginning of the 18th century. At that time, no progress was made, the nation soon after vanquishing those who might have been intent on attacking the yard. Matters were much altered by the middle years of the century, however, with the scheme once again under consideration during the time of the Seven Years War. In 1755, a Board of Ordnance planner, Hugh Debbeig, produced a viable scheme of fortifications that involved the construction of a series of ditches and ramparts, the ditches to be 27ft. wide and 8ft. deep. Before the Lines could be cut, land already acquired by Acts of Parliament passed in 1708 and 1709 had to be cleared of those who had been allowed to continue leasing it for the grazing of animals. Once construction began, John Desmontze of the Royal Engineers supervised progress. Subsequently known as the Cumberland or Chatham Lines, this ambitious project stretched from just east of the gun wharf out towards Gillingham, where it enclosed the community of

Brompton, before returning to the river and terminating at a point north-west of the dock-yard. The first phase of these works was completed in 1758, and additions and improvements were undertaken later in the century.

It was these improved defences that prompted construction of the first purpose-built military accommodation within the area. Located inside the defended area of the Lines, close to the parish boundary with Gillingham, was Chatham Barracks. Construction work began in 1757, and the first regiment moved into these quarters in 1760. The barracks, at that time, consisted of blocks large enough to house two infantry battalions and two companies of foot artillery, while there was also a separate infirmary block for the sick. As might be expected, the erection of these buildings turned Chatham into an important billeting centre, to which regiments were now sent simply because of the existence of barracks. The Chatham Company of the Royal Artificers was primarily responsible for the Lines, and other regiments, while

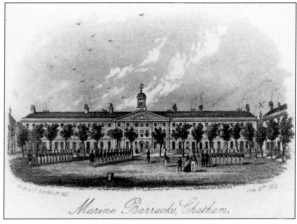

39 The Marine barracks at Chatham were completed some time around 1779. At the far right end of this building was the sergeants' mess, and a dining room occupied the upper floor. Note the clock, the significance of which is revealed in a later chapter.

38 A great many clues to Chatham's past are to be found in the grounds that surround the parish church. Some of the burial stones relate to naval and dockyard inhabitants of the town. This stone marks the passing of John King, Master House Carpenter of Sheerness dockyard. King had also served in a more junior capacity at Chatham yard.

performing duties on the Lines, were there largely for purposes of accommodation.[21] By 1780, in fact, barrack accommodation had become a serious problem, and proposals were put forward to turn nearby Rochester Castle into military accommodation at a cost of £3,000.[22] These proposals were turned down and it was not until 1804 that the problem was eventually solved with the building of new barracks at Brompton. In 1806, the Chatham Company of the Royal Military Artificers was transferred there.[23]

Unrelated to the Army barracks was the provision of further accommodation for the Navy's own soldiers, the sea-borne Marines. These barracks, which were also situated alongside Dock Road were begun in 1777, with occupancy taking

place two years later. The following divisional order of the Marines was issued on 2 September 1779:

> The Marine Barracks being so far forward as to be fit to receive some of the Division, to inhabit these rooms proper for that purpose, it is therefore the Commanding Officer's directions that as many of those of the Division now at Quarters as the said Barracks may contain, shall march in on Friday afternoon, thereto remain to lodge and inhabit until further orders.[24]

The Chatham Division of the Marines had a personnel at this time of not less than 4,000, though the number billeted at Chatham would rarely approach this figure. As might be expected, detachments were constantly at sea, with only limited numbers remaining on land. In fact, the Marine Barracks, as built, had accommodation for only 600, with additional numbers billeted at various public houses.

The large military and naval presence within the parish helps explain a seeming peculiarity of the 1801 census. For Chatham, the printed returns show women making up 55 per cent of the population, while the parish burial registers

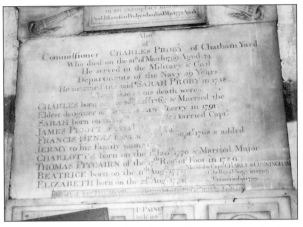

40 A victualling yard once stood at the west end of the High Street. This memorial in the parish church records the name of Milbourne Marsh, one time agent victualler.

41 Another memorial in the parish church records the passing of Charles Proby, one of the longer serving dockyard commissioners. He held the office from 22 October 1771 until his death in March 1799.

appear to suggest a male population well in excess of females: in any one year there were nearly twice as many men buried as women. The reasons for this seeming anomaly are simple. Within the census returns all reference to military personnel stationed in the area was omitted, but this was not the case with parish records. In fact, as might be expected, the registers carry a large number of references to the military. In 1781, for instance, a not unusual year, 22 per cent of all burials were serving members of the Army. As for the higher proportion of women making up the non-military population of Chatham, a number of factors attracted them into the parish. Many, of course, were the wives and daughters of those who already resided in the area, while others were related to serving members of the Army or Navy. Chatham being a manning port, ships frequently returned to the dockyard, where wives were then allowed on board. With regard to the Marines, the situation

is slightly harder to assess, for many wives were given accommodation within the Marine barracks. When this was the case they, too, were excluded from the census return. If their husbands were posted away, wives could only remain in the barracks for a further period of six months.

In addition to wives, there were numerous prostitutes living in the town of Chatham. The dockyard towns had a notorious reputation for the number of brothels they harboured, with young girls sometimes attracted into the area from the surrounding countryside. Specific evidence for Chatham is sparse, but there can be little doubt that prostitution here, as elsewhere, was extremely well organised. Further, it was not unusual for groups of women to travel to particular dockyard towns when a ship was known to be de-commissioning. Again, this probably happened at Chatham, with local bum boatmen more than prepared to row them out.[25]

Five

Town Improvements

Mr. Douglas, in his *Nenia Britannica*, has published his observations on the various Roman remains discovered within these lines at different times, with several engravings of the Tumuli opened, and the contents found in them.

Edward Hasted (1798)

In the year 1770, attention was again given to the massive defensive undertaking known as the Chatham Lines. The original line of defences formed a tight ring around the dockyard and gun wharf, and it was now decided to push these out further to the north and east. Based on a plan laid down by Lt.-General Skinner, the north-west extension of the Lines would now take the fortifications to St Mary's Creek, strengthening the dockyard from an attack on this side. As for the eastward extension, this would take the line of fortifications out towards Rochester, where Fort Clarence (1812) and Fort Pitt (1819) would eventually be built. At the same time, the original Lines were to be re-modelled with the addition of a redoubt complex that would become known as Fort Amherst.[1] During construction of these works, Chatham Barracks was extended; this eventually had accommodation for 2,000 soldiers. In enlarging the barracks, further land had to be acquired on Chatham Hill, which led to the demolition of the government-owned Hill House.

The soldiers engaged in creating the ditches and embankments that made up the Chatham Lines were often surprised by what their spades and picks uncovered. Frequently they came across decayed bones, rusting swords and the occasional coin showing the face of a Roman emperor. Unfortunately, in building the Lines, the Army was desecrating an area of considerable historical importance, the whole of the Lines seemingly covered with countless barrows and levelled graves, most of them belonging to Anglo-Saxon settlers of the 5th and 6th centuries. Much of this material would have been lost to us if it had not been for one rather fortuitous appointment. In 1779, Captain James Douglas was ordered to join the

staff of Lt.-Colonel Debbeig, who, in 1778, had been appointed Chief Engineer.

Douglas had a considerable interest in the past and was clearly excited by the various artifacts constantly brought to his attention. He remembered a massive collection of bones, teeth and tusks that had been discovered six years earlier. Uncovered during the digging of foundations for a storehouse, it was at first assumed they belonged to one of the elephants brought to Britain by the Emperor Hadrian; Douglas suggested they belonged to a hippopotamus, and went on to propose that such animals had once freely roamed the river beds of ancient Chatham. He was as far from the truth as the elephant hypothesists had been, but he did provide a number of careful drawings. From these it is possible to suggest that the bones belonged to a mammoth, a creature that most certainly did roam the Medway area some 10,000 years ago.

Over the following decade or so, Douglas was to supervise the excavation of more than a hundred historical sites in the Chatham area. Of particular importance was the uncovering, in 1782, of a Roman building during construction of the Amherst redoubt. In a paper that Douglas subsequently gave before the Society of Antiquaries, he claimed this to have been the headquarters of the Commander of the Saxon Shore. Such a conclusion is less than likely, although the building, which measured 12ft. by 18ft. and contained several small rooms, may have had a military connection. It was probably an Army outpost designed to provide some form of defence for the Medway crossing. Support for this is given by the discovery of a similar building on the far side of the river.[2]

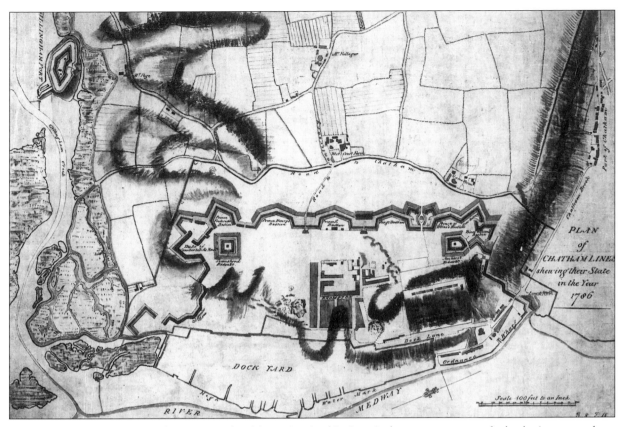

42   The Chatham defensive lines as completed by 1786. At this time Amherst was a mere redoubt, having yet to be developed into a fully fledged fort.

43   The Barrier Gate. Without this gateway, the new defensive lines would have isolated the dockyard from nearby Chatham town. The Barrier Gate was fitted with stout timber doors while the approach road was covered by loop holes for riflemen.

44   An interior view of the impressive defences that now make up Fort Amherst.

45 Fort Amherst during the 19th century was frequently the venue for a number of large-scale military exercises, although no actual fighting took place.

46 In more recent years, Fort Amherst has been developed as a tourist attraction. Every so often an army, representing 'Napoleonic France', is allowed to borrow the Fort.

While the various prehistoric and Roman remains are of importance, it is the numerous burial mounds of the Anglo-Saxon period that are of greatest importance. Indeed, within these graves were found both the skeletal remains and some of the more precious possessions of the Jutish settlers who first created the village of Chatham.[3] On a site close to St Mary's Church, for instance, in a grave opened in 1782, the remains of a woman were revealed. Alongside her were various items of jewellery together with a coin of Anthemius, Emperor of the West, A.D. 467-72. A second tumulus, near the scarp of the hill which faces St Mary's Church and opened on 10 August 1782, was also found to contain a Roman coin, this one stamped with the face of II Valentian (AD375-392). The discovery of these and other coins led at one time to the suggestion that these burials were of 'Romanized Britons'.[4] However, there is little else which points to such a conclusion, these early Chatham settlers having no more than loose trading connections with the remnants of the Empire. The various other tumuli that Douglas uncovered contained, apart from coins, such items as crystal beads (tumulus VI), arrow heads (IX), an iron bow brace (X), silver gilt fibulous (XII) and amber and glass beads (XIX).[5]

Douglas kept extensive notes on his various discoveries, and later ensured their wider availability through publication of his *Nenia Britannica* in 1793. As well as extensive references and drawings of the artifacts discovered at Chatham, the book includes considerable material from numerous other sites, much further afield. The Chatham finds are crucial to the publication, though, with a plan of a barrow on Chatham Lines forming the frontispiece of the book and constituting one of the earliest illustrations of English archaeology in the field. As for the artifacts which were uncovered, many are now to be found in the Ashmolean Museum, Oxford.[6]

Interesting developments were also taking place within the area of the actual town at the same time. Of particular importance was the establishment of a commission that was to take responsibility for 'the better Paving, Cleansing, Lighting and Watching' of the streets of Chatham. Given legal authority by an Act of Parliament passed in 1772, the commissioners were also responsible for overseeing construction of the Chatham section of New Road. The factor that

47 On the following day, and somewhat predictably, the Fort is recaptured by British red coats.

48 Considerable rebuilding work was underway in the dockyard during the late 18th century. In particular, the ropery was reconstructed in brick. The main ropehouse, seen here, was completed in 1791.

49 Graffiti to be found on one of the ropeyard buildings. The earliest appears to date to 1788. All would have been made there by dockyard workers (or their apprentices).

had prompted this move was nearby Rochester's acquisition of a similar act three years earlier, resulting in a number of improvements to the City that made it considerably more attractive than Chatham. In fact, by adding lighting and improving the walkways of Rochester High Street, the dirt and dinginess of Chatham had been considerably emphasised. This led to the fear that Chatham would be avoided by travellers who would consider the town to be 'unsafe and disagreeable'.[7]

The problem was that prior to this act nobody had taken any real responsibility for ensuring that the town of Chatham was a pleasant place in which to live. Admittedly, the vestry had given thought to street cleaning, and references to occasional contracts are to be found in the minutes of their meetings. In 1722, for instance, William Brotherstone was employed in this task,

> that the said William Brotherstone shall and will at his own proper cost and charge take up and carry away all the Soile and Dirt in the streets of Chatham from Hangmans Lane one side of the way to the gate of Sir John Hawkins' Hospital from thence on both sides of the way to the pound and all Globe Lane, for which its ordered that the overseers of the poor shall pay the said William Brotherstone the sum of twenty pounds ...[8]

However, the clearing of the High Street, even if undertaken regularly, was only a partial solution. To improve the quality of life within the town something would have to be done about a number of other problems. Among these were a rising crime rate, lack of street lighting and a High Street that was frequently impassable because of the volume of horse-drawn traffic attempting to squeeze through.

It was in an attempt to address these various problems that a group of the more affluent and influential town dwellers came together. Taking their lead from Rochester, who had obtained their Act of Parliament only three years earlier, they drew up a similar bill. Once passed, this allowed them to levy the necessary rates for the employment of night watchmen, street cleaners and lamp lighters. Along the length of the High Street, a set of oil lamps was placed in position, while at certain strategic points a number of watch boxes was erected for use by night watchmen. These same individuals were also given a specific area to patrol, their task that of ensuring the safe passage

of those whose legitimate affairs took them out during the hours of darkness. The commissioners who were appointed to oversee this work undertook the task with apparent alacrity, and Edward Hasted was able to write only a decade or so after the passing of the Parliamentary Act,

> the High-Street has been new paved and lighted, and several of the annoyances have been removed, which before rendered this narrow thoroughfare so inconvenient and disagreeable to passengers; the expenses of which are raised on proprietors of houses and lands, by a rate not exceeding ninepence in the pound.[9]

Not all areas of Chatham, however, benefited from these improvements. They were restricted only to those areas of the town that housed the most affluent. Poorer areas, such as Smithfield Banks, were specifically excluded, those who lived there deemed too poor to pay the new rate. As such, those areas declined further, making Chatham into a town marked by huge social differences.

Among those who worked especially hard on behalf of improvements to Chatham was the highly influential James Best. Born in 1720, he had succeeded his father, Mawdistley Best, as head of the brewing company that was centred on the north side of the High Street, alongside Manor Road. As such, the Bests were an established Chatham family and one that frequently took an interest in the affairs of the town. In 1664, Thomas Best, who was probably founder of the company, was a leading member of the vestry and held office as surveyor of the highways. In turn his son, also Thomas, was one of the subscribers that gave money for the building of the workhouse.

In managing the family business, James Best sought to keep pace with the latest ideas pioneered by other companies, while bringing about numerous improvements to his own product. Inventories of the firm dating from 1754 and 1763 show that, between these dates, several important items of equipment were introduced to keep pace with expanded production. The first of these inventories shows that six pumps were owned by the company (variously named 'wort pumps', 'jigger pumps', 'copper pumps' and 'hand pumps') while the latter inventory reveals the number of pumps to have increased to 11 (including a 'force liquer pump', a 'wooden pump' and several 'cleansing pumps'). As further evidence of the expansion of the company during this period, James Best had increased the size of his business property, the lease of a storehouse at Sun Quay being taken on in 1775, while a malt house, mill house and stable were added four years later. In 1772, it is recorded, the company used 23,000 barrels of malt and hops, with suppliers including Mitchell of Gillingham and William Finch of Rainham. By the mid-century period James Best was distributing beer to over ninety inns and taverns, more than forty of which were situated within the town of Chatham.

On the death of James Best in 1782, the company was valued at approximately £60,000. This was considerably in excess of its value some thirty years earlier and the result of his sound business acumen. Unfortunately, those who followed him showed much less enthusiasm, the company running into financial difficulty. The two sons of James Best who inherited the business took more out of the company than they put in, and the family solicitors, William and Edward Twopenny, had to step in and run the company on their behalf. Despite such misfortune, the company had consolidated James Best's earlier policy of acquiring tied houses, with 65

freeholds and 16 leaseholds held by the company in 1793. That James Best, even in the final years of his life, continued to give thought both to his company and the affairs of Chatham, is borne out by his will. In this document he bequeathed £200 for the enlargement and improvement of the workhouse.[10]

The death of James Best was a sad loss to the town. No doubt his enthusiasm and leadership qualities were sorely missed just four years later, when it was determined that the old parish church needed to be demolished. The problem was that St Mary's had begun life as a small village church and was no longer capable of meeting the needs of a town that had a population in excess of 6,000. Admittedly, in previous years, the church had been enlarged. In 1635, for example, the Navy Board, as the dockyard did not have a chapel, had paid a large sum towards the repair of the church. At the same time, they rebuilt and enlarged the west end while also paying for the construction of a steeple. Similarly, in 1707, the Resident Commissioner of the dockyard, George St Loe, had financed the building of a gallery over the south aisle. This provided the church with at least fifty

50 St Mary's Church as it appeared towards the end of the 18th century. The west end had been reconstructed earlier in the century with much of the rest of the church rebuilt during the 1780s.

51 A chapel was constructed in the dockyard between 1808 and 1811. Costing £9,000, it was partly designed to offset the growth of non conformity among dockyard employees.

52 This sign suggests that the chapel was built by French wartime prisoners, but there is little evidence for this statement.

new sittings. However, such piecemeal enlargements were no longer able to meet the growing needs of such a vibrant parish. In many respects there was only one solution, the complete rebuilding of the church. The first reference in a vestry meeting to this possibility appears to have been in August 1746. On that occasion, those attending were told that the church was 'in great danger of falling and that the Parishioners cannot attend divine service therein without running the hazard of their lives'. A full survey of the building was immediately ordered, those carrying out the survey being informed that they might give thought to the entire demolition of the building. In the event, such a radical solution was not adopted, although extensive alterations and improvements were introduced. At a vestry meeting held in September 1746 it was

> Resolved that the old roof of the church be taken off and the old pillars be taken down and the North and South walls be raised for a Span roof and there be a Gallery built against the North wall & the chancel Roof to be new framed & there be proper drawings & drafts & proposals of scantlings & Dimensions for the several workmen in order for the bringing an estimate for carrying on & finishing the same ...[11]

Further thought to a complete rebuilding of the church came in 1786. On that occasion, a special committee, consisting of 20 leading members of the community, was established. Dominating their thoughts was the fact that a larger church would need to be situated in a less restricted area. The recent military developments had considerably reduced the space surrounding the church, neighbouring land now containing various fortifications and the new barracks. In addition, the government was keen to add a series of further structures in this same area. For this reason, the War Office showed a willingness to offer an alternative site for the church—at the south end of Dock Road and immediately next to the fortified gateway entrance that cut across the Lines. This particular gateway, constructed of brick, was known as the Barrier Gate and had been added by Hugh Debbeig in order to permit easy access to Gillingham and Brompton villages as well as to the church and dockyard. Without this gateway through the Lines, the dockyard and the village of Brompton would have been completely cut off from Chatham.

This scheme for the entire reconstruction of the church came extremely close to fruition. A subscription list was drawn up and architectural plans prepared. In the event, however, the majority of vestry members were uncertain as to the advantages of such a scheme. At a ballot, held in the vestry rooms on 2 December 1786, a total of 426 members of the congregation cast their vote. Of this number, 298 (70 per cent) voted against the scheme. According to the special committee that had been set up to consider the proposal, it was felt that the majority of parishioners were influenced by the supposedly high costs. Most, it seems, were unaware of a 'liberal subscription to the amount of nineteen hundred pounds', which meant that, instead of adding three shillings in the pound to the church rate, the actual amount would be only one shilling. Following the ballot, the committee adjourned '*sine die*', having decided that the question of building a new church was dead.

Something, had still to be done about the existing building, of course, it being both too small and in need of repair. An alternative scheme was now proposed, retaining the enlarged and recently improved west end; only the nave and chancel were to be demolished and replaced by a wider and larger structure. This also allowed for the addition of an extended gallery that was to run the complete length of the nave on both its south and north sides. In keeping with the fashion of the period, the new work was finished in the classical style and does not appear to be dissimilar to the dockyard chapel that was completed a few years later.

Both Baptists and Congregationalists had long been established in the town, a Zion Baptist chapel having been built in 1644, followed by the Congregationalist Ebenezer chapel of 1648 in Meeting House Lane. However, it was the rapid growth of Methodism during the 18th century that had the greatest impact upon the church of St Mary's, a number of worshippers choosing to transfer their allegiance to a chapel built in 1770. Methodism initially took root among those employed in the dockyard, but Wesley's first visit to Chatham saw him preaching to a small group assembled in the barracks. This was on 28 December 1768, the room set aside for the purpose having a bedstead that doubled as a pulpit. Some four weeks later, Wesley was again in Chatham, this time

53   Interior view of the dockyard chapel.

preaching to an open-air meeting in Clover Street. By 1775, the Chatham Wesleyans had 112 members, a large number still drawn from those serving in the Army or employed in the dockyard. This part of Chatham was something of a centre for local non-conformity with both an Ebenezer Chapel and a Zion Chapel established in Clover Street during the late 18th century.[12] The government's concern at the growth of Methodism was part of the reason that a separate chapel was built in the dockyard.

In the meantime, Chatham's population continued to increase, even accelerating in its rate of growth. In 1767, those responsible for administering the poor rate assessed a total of 1,255 properties, suggesting a population of 5,600. By 1801, however, when the first census was taken, the town's civilian population had reached the figure of 10,505. In this 34-year period there would appear to have been an 87 per cent increase. This, of course, is a fairly considerable growth rate, being much higher than at any time during the previous half century, and it might, quite justifiably, be claimed that the figure, in some way, is inflated. After all, poor rate assessments were never designed to show population size, while the 1801 census returns are notoriously inaccurate. Additional evidence would seem to suggest, however, that this was not an unlikely growth rate. The church registers certainly show a marked increase in activity levels during this period; the baptismal records indicate an increase of 73 per cent from the year 1767 until the end of the century, while the number of baptisms doubled. More important, though, are the later and more accurate census returns which confirm a similar rate of population increase. Between 1811 and 1841, for instance, the total population rose by 66 per cent, while for the period 1801 to 1831 there was a growth rate of 64 per cent.[13]

Analysis of church records for the period 1770 to 1801 opens up the possibility of gauging the years in which this acceleration occurred. Detailed below are the decennial average figures for baptisms over the period 1770 to 1799. The years after 1780 show a particularly high level of growth:

Decennial Period	Average number of baptisms per year
1770-1779	301.8
1780-1789	393
1790-1799	466[14]

Marriage records also confirm that the 1780s was the period in which this accelerated population growth took place:

Decennial Period	Average number of marriages per year
1770-1779	80.6
1780-1789	103.7
1790-1799	112.2[15]

Undoubtedly, a major contributor to this population growth was the industrial-military complexes. During the 20 years between 1775 and 1795, the dockyard expanded its work force by 25 per cent and the victualling yard by some 30 per cent.

Year	Nos. Employed
1775	1,456
1780	1,599
1785	1,646
1790	1,650
1795	1,827[16]

For Chatham, the end of the 18th century proved to be a time of upheaval and discontent. Primarily this was caused by a further period of war with France. Many in the town were opposed to the war, seeing it as a drain on the nation's resources. One Chatham publican, for example, displayed on his mantelpiece the words, 'national debt £75 a minute, sleeping or waking'.[17] In fact, by the end of the war, the national debt had grown from £228m to £876m, an increase of £58 'a minute, sleeping or waking'. The war affected the poor and disadvantaged far more than any other sector of the population. They were the ones who had to meet the massive increase in food prices that war created. During 1795, the second full year of war, wheat prices had rocketed by a staggering 44 per cent, leading to riots throughout the country. In Chatham, the weekly market witnessed attacks upon butchers, the crowd insisting that they sell 'their meat at four pence per pound'.[18]

Within the dock and victualling yards there was further discontent, with both sets of workers demanding an increase in their pay to cover the increasing costs to which they were being put. At the time of the market riots, the entire force of 600 dockyard shipwrights was on strike. Earlier, in 1792, Jacobinism had been present in the yard, with the shipwright Thomas Burton dismissed from the service when he was discovered selling copies of Thomas Paine's *Rights of Man*.[19] At the same time, a fire on board a warship in dry dock had been accompanied by a seditious note that threatened 'More Wages or More Fires', while at the same time a slogan on the dockyard wall proclaimed 'No Taxes, No Kings'.[20] For the authorities, however, the most worrying example of dockyard militancy took place in 1801, when the entire 2000-strong work force combined not only with those at the victualling yard but also those employed in all other naval facilities throughout the country.[21] Their united aim was that of an improvement in wages, with the Navy Board agreeing to a special war-time payment.[22]

Six

Our Parish

It is like most seaports, a long narrow, disagreeable, ill-built town, the houses in general occupied by those trades adapted to the commerce of the shipping and seafaring person, the Victualling Office, and the two breweries being the only tolerably built houses in it.

Hasted (1798).

The year 1800 brought to Chatham a period of extraordinary fine weather. The summer months of May and June saw days of endless sunshine and hardly a drop of rain. Yet such weather could hardly have been welcomed. The effect on the central residential area would have been quite unbearable. In the many small, poorly built and ill-ventilated houses that made up the township of Chatham, the occupants suffered greatly. Once they closed the outside door behind them, they were immersed in the fetid and malodorous environment that such housing created. In the summer of 1800 it was made ten times worse by the unusually high temperatures.

Nor did the streets provide any form of respite. Lacking a heavy downpour, they were infrequently cleaned. In particular, the gutters and side walks were tainted with foul-smelling human effluent and other indescribable deposits. Not surprisingly, the danger of disease was rife. In that year, the burial registers recorded 442 deaths. This represented a death rate of approximately forty in every thousand and so made Chatham one of the unhealthiest towns in Kent. The average life expectancy of those living in the town was no more than 30 years.

This long spell of hot weather brought other concerns. Many of the houses built in central Chatham were of timber construction; as each day passed, the lack of rain endangered the combustible nature of the building material. The slightest accident, be it from an unattended candle or a misused tinder-box, might lead to an uncontrollable fire. Already, once in that year, the threat had become near-reality when, towards the end of May, a new iron foundry had caught fire. That the conflagration had not spread was due to

the foundry being next to the victualling yard. Those employed within the naval establishment had reacted to the danger, rapidly bringing their fire engines to the scene. Although the foundry was entirely destroyed, the fire was prevented from spreading.

On the last day of June, however, the town was not so fortunate. Shortly before mid-day, a serious fire broke out in a small warehouse that stood behind the High Street and immediately adjacent to the river. The contents of the warehouse, a highly combustible combination of oakum, cordage and hemp, burst into flames, with the entire building soon engulfed. Everything seemed to favour the fire. The warehouse was of timber construction and newly coated with tar, while surrounding houses were also of timber and bone dry as a result of the recent hot weather. The fire broke out about an hour before the ebb tide, and it was virtually impossible for the arriving fire engines to draw water. Furthermore, a number

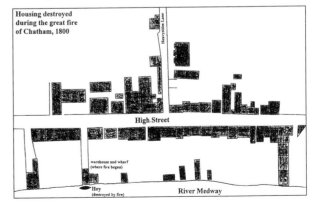

54 Plan of the High Street areas devastated by the great fire of 1800.

55   A section of Chatham High Street that escaped the fires of both 1800 and 1820. This early 20th-century photograph reveals the combustible nature of the buildings that once fronted the High Street.

of hoys which were tied to a nearby quay were unable to escape and were also caught in the conflagration.

Over the next three hours, nearly one hundred buildings on both the north and south sides of the High Street were entirely destroyed by the fire. Over a hundred people were forced to flee the blaze, most of them taking to the adjoining fields and roads for safety. Here, also, were brought various items of furniture and other belongings, many of them snatched from the flames that were ready to engulf any precious belongings.

That the fire was eventually brought under control was once again due to the Navy's presence in the area. From the dockyard, Commissioner Hartwell dispatched all of the yard fire engines together with numerous butts of water. He also released the entire workforce, arming them with pikes that they might help in the pulling down of buildings for the creation of a firebreak. Similarly, fire engines and butts of water were dispatched from the much nearer victualling yard. All these joined a hard-pressed parish engine and those belonging to the Best Company Brewery. Troops from the Marine and Chatham barracks were also ordered to the scene, many of them helping in the task of removing furniture from houses threatened by the fire. They also formed a guard that prevented the less scrupulous from stealing these same items of property. Unfortunately, theft during a fire was quite common, those involved known as 'fire priggers'.

56 Chatham, viewed from the heights of Fort Amherst, 1832, a general view based on a study by the landscape artist J.M.W. Turner. It is from here that a military guard was first to report the fire of 1820.

Loss of life was mercifully small. Unfortunately, though, there were four victims. Among them was a servant to the influential Best family, William Bassett, who, despite entreaties and remonstrances, rushed back to his burning house to collect some money he had left. It was at this point that the house collapsed, and Bassett was buried under the ruins. Elsewhere, after the fire had subsided, a Mrs. Dunk and her babe in arms were killed by a chimney that fell from the roof of a fire-wrecked house.

The local community soon came to the aid of those who had suffered. While some had the fortune to be insured, the vast majority had nothing to fall back on. The fire had taken much of their wealth while leaving them homeless. From Chatham barracks, Major-General Hewett sent tents for those who had no other accommodation. These were pitched in a field adjoining New Road. Of particular significance was the holding of a public meeting some three days later. Here it was resolved that a committee should be

established and a collection made 'for the immediate relief of the unfortunate sufferers'.

The notes kept by the committee are of considerable value to the historian. They provide a cross-section of Chatham housing, and its population, at this point in time. According to the notes kept by William Jeffreys, the fire actually affected 97 separate properties, variously consisting of both dwelling and lodging houses. All were of timber construction. While a number of houses were occupied by only one family, there were also, within the compact area of the fire, a number of much larger properties that had been subject to tenementing. Among families listed as living in untenemented houses the head of the household is often stated to have been an artisan; surprisingly, there is also a number of labourers in untenemented houses.[1] The social mix of the area is futher demonstrated by a brief reference to the north side of the High Street which is characterised by a marked degree of affluence. Here, for instance, were several slightly larger houses that contained a single family and their many servants. On this side of the High Street there was also The Trumpet, a lodging house of the better type. Among its occupants were two women, both of substance, together with three well-placed artisans: a blacksmith, shipwright and housecarpenter.[2]

As well as containing the comfortable and spacious housing of artisans, better-off labourers and members of the middle class, Chatham High Street also contained a small number of tenemented properties that suffered from over-crowding. Situated mainly to the south, one such house, admittedly larger than most, was sub-divided into 10 separate units, which housed 15 adults and 10 children. These tenemented properties stretched from the Mount to Heavyside Lane. Here, they abruptly terminated. Heavyside Lane itself contained nine properties. All were occupied as single units that housed, among others, a 67-year-old labourer, a bricklayer's labourer, a widow of 66 years and another of 70 (both living in the same house), a slopfeller and an ordinaryman.[3]

From the notes collected by the committee, it is clear that not all artisans and labourers of Chatham were subject to the severe overcrowding of the industrial towns of the north. Many were accommodated in through-terraced housing and did not suffer the inconvenience of sharing with others. Indeed, those who lived away from the High Street were often lucky in that they also had small gardens and looked out on open spaces of ground. The High Street, of course, was somewhat more heavily populated, with breaks in development only occurring when a second road or walkway was reached. Increasingly though, even land sited away from the High Street was becoming subjected to in-filling, several back-to-back houses having been introduced.[4] As elsewhere, such residences, with their lack of light and ventilation, meant that an extremely unhygienic atmosphere was created.

A more general look at the entire parish will give us an indication of the state of the area together with some idea of the vast changes that were then taking place. The starting point for an imaginary walk will be the extreme west end of the High Street at that point which connects with Rochester. The first group of buildings to be seen are those of the victualling yard. This stands on the north side of the street and ran down to

the edge of the river. Edward Hasted, writing in the 1790s, provided this description of the yard:

> At the entrance of Chatham from Rochester, on the north side of the High-street is the Victualling-office, for the use of the royal navy lying here, at Sheerness, and the Nore. In it there is a cooperage, pickling, baking, cutting, slaughter, and store-houses. A new wharf has been lately made to it, and additional buildings erected for the further convenience and service of the victualling. This office is under the management of an agent victualler, and a store-keeper.[5]

Although the victualling yard was particularly busy at this time, it was soon to see a reversal of its fortunes. At the end of the Napoleonic Wars, in 1815, it saw a considerable reduction in the size of the workforce. By 1820, the number employed had been reduced to four and the yard finally closed in 1826.[6]

St Bartholomew's Hospital had been located on the south side of the High Street and close to the victualling yard. However, the majority of the buildings that once belonged to the hospital had now been replaced by private housing, with only the chapel still remaining. Given the extensive alterations that were made to this same building during the late-Victorian period, Hasted's description of the building as it then existed is useful:

> The most ancient part is the east end, which is probably the remains of the original structure, which was erected by Hugh de Trottesclyve, a monk of Rochester, in the time of Henry I for the use of the lepers, and dedicated by him to St Bartholomew. It is a small circus, having three narrow Gothic windows, and is built and roofed with stone; hence a chancel extends to the west, which, though ancient, does not appear of equal antiquity with the others.[7]

In 1743, an extension to the chapel had been added, paid for by the then lord of the manor, William Walter. He also added a number of pews. In 1800, services were still provided for those who lived some distance from the church of St Mary's.

It was also the task of the chaplain appointed to St Bartholomew's to preach every Sunday in the chapel attached to Sir John Hawkins' Hospital. This was the building that stood immediately opposite the chapel and which served as a retreat 'for poor decayed mariners and shipwrights'.[8] The condition of many of the dwelling houses that stood within the grounds of the hospital had fallen into decay, and in 1780 a plan had been devised by the governors of the hospital entirely to replace many of the older buildings. It was at this point, also, that a new entrance was constructed giving access to the hospital direct from the High Street. According to the accounts held by the governors, the cost of reconstructing the hospital amounted to £1,189 6s. 7d. This outlay might have been higher had it not been for a scheme put forward by George Pemble, a carpenter, who demolished and rebuilt one of the houses on the estate at his own cost. The building concerned was a large house that was owned by the charity and stood immediately alongside the hospital. In carrying out this work, George Pemble gained the right to a 40-year lease on the house, commencing on Michaelmas Day 1790.

It is only a short walk along the High Street before the area which was devastated by the fire is reached. Past the blackened remains of the destroyed properties, a large brick building is soon approached. This is Chatham House, erected by James Best in 1742 as a family dwelling. The construction of the house in this situation, on the edge of the family-owned brewery, reflected the owners' need to be permanently available to manage the expanding business.

Although Chatham House survived the fire (it was only slightly damaged), a second horrendous fire was responsible for its complete destruction. On 3 March 1820, a fire in a High Street bakehouse rapidly spread to a number of surrounding buildings. In all, a total of 34 dwelling houses and 13 warehouses, all located between Heavyside Lane and Manor Road, were entirely destroyed. In contrast to the earlier fire, a number of those who gave the appearance of helping to save property turned out to be fire priggers. One of them, Lamont Wilson, a soldier from Chatham Barracks, was sentenced to a long term of imprisonment as a result of entering Chatham House and removing for his own purposes a razor case and looking glass. Several other individuals, similarly charged, found their names reported in a subsequent edition of the *Kentish Gazette*:

James Griffin was found <u>guilty</u> of stealing earthenware, the property of Humphrey

Wickham. Nicholas Ash was also found <u>Guilty</u> of stealing several bottles of wine, the property of Richard Winch, on March 3rd. The prisoner was seen coming out of the cellar with the property. Daniel Dowd was likewise found <u>Guilty</u> of stealing tickling [linen bedding] &tc. on the same occasion. He had it tied up in a bundle, and was stopped when crossing the bridge, by the soldiers.[9]

Following the fire of 1820, a committee of relief was again established, which gave consideration to the needs of those who had suffered. On this occasion, the committee consisted of 32 notables belonging to the parish. Included in this number was a certain John Dickens, a pay clerk in the dockyard. He had first moved to Chatham in 1817, having been transferred to the dockyard from Somerset House. His family moved into a recently built three-storey building that stood in Ordnance Terrace, with splendid views across the town of Chatham and towards the open land that made up the Lines.

In all, John Dickens had eight children, the second of whom was named Charles. This frail youngster was to grow into the nation's most famous novelist. Furthermore, it was the young boy's brief stay in the parish of Chatham that was to provide the future writer with a number of ideas that he packed into those novels. Of childhood games, for instance, such as those played in the cornfields (now the railway station) that stood opposite the family house, Charles Dickens later recalled:

57 The Chatham dockyard pay office, where John Dickens, the father of the famous novelist, was briefly employed.

58 Ordnance Terrace, a group of three-storey buildings, into which the Dickens family moved in 1817.

Here, in the haymaking time had I been delivered from the dungeons of Seringapatam, an immense pile [of haycock], by my own countrymen, the victorious British (boy next door and his two cousins) and had been recognised with ectasy by my affianced one (Miss Green), who had come all the way from England (second house in the terrace) to ransom me and marry me.[10]

Other memories which Dickens took from Chatham, a town described by his friend and biographer, John Forster, as 'the birthplace of his fancy', were the dingy and overcrowded streets, various horrific tales from the workhouse (including that of a boy who asked for more) and a general view of life in the dockyard. *Great Expectations* is a good example of the use to which he put some of those memories. Although not written until 1861, by which time Dickens had returned to the area after a long period of absence, there can be little doubt that the song 'Old Clem' had stuck in his mind since childhood visits to his father's dockyard office. It was, in fact, a song once sung by the yard anchor smiths:

There was a song that Joe used to hum fragments of at the forge, of which the burden was Old Clem. This was not a very ceremonious way of rendering homage to a patron saint; but I believe Old Clem stood in that relation towards smiths. It was a song that imitated the measure of beating upon iron, and was a mere lyrical excuse for the introduction of Old Clem's respected name.

59 As a result of financial difficulties, the result of profligacy, the Dickens family were forced to move to the Brook in 1821—then the least desirable section of Chatham. The house, 18 St Mary's Place, was demolished in 1943.

60 Part of a stone dock within the dockyard. Numerous convicts were employed on its construction during the second decade of the 19th century, and it was the sight of them that probably led to the creation of Magwitch in *Great Expectations*.

> Thus, you were to hammer boys round—Old Clem! With a thump and a sound—Old Clem! Beat it out, beat it out—Old Clem! With a clink for the stout—Old Clem! Blow the fire, blow the fire—Old Clam! Roaring drier, soaring higher Old Clem![11]

It is likely that Magwitch, the celebrated convict, also originated from those early dockyard days, for, as the young Charles Dickens wandered freely around the yard, he would have come across a number of convicted felons whose sentence of hard labour had brought them to Chatham for the purpose of building a new dry dock.

The Dickens family were to live in Ordnance Terrace for about four years. In 1821, they were forced to find cheaper accommodation when John Dickens entered a period of financial crisis. In fact, he was quite incapable of handling money and would eventually be incarcerated in a debtors' prison. For this reason, John Dickens is usually regarded as the man upon whom the reckless spendthrift Wilkins Micawber was later to be modelled.

The second Chatham home of the Dickens family was 18 St Mary's Place. No longer in existence, having been demolished in 1943, it was a small cottage situated in the Brook. This was the poorest area in the whole of Chatham, the quality of life made worse by the existence nearby of a fetid stream (always referred to as the brook) which took most of the town's effluent.

Shortly after moving to St Mary's Place, Charles Dickens' father was recalled to the Navy Office in London, resulting in the future novelist eventually bidding farewell to his boyhood home. The journey to London, another event that was to be used in future books, involved his conveyance in a stage coach '... melodiously called "Timpson's Blue Eyed Maid" '. In fact, the coach was owned by Mr. Simpson. His offices in Chatham High Street were the starting point for two London-bound stages, departing at 6 a.m. and 8.30 a.m.

Once we get past Chatham House, much of the continuing length of the High Street has on the south side an estate belonging to the Best family. The brewery has already been mentioned. Beyond that, however, was a pleasant area of ground made up of cherry orchards, a meadow and pasture land. The tremendous demand for housing had eventually encouraged the sons of James Best to develop this land for housing, and a series of streets, many of them interconnecting with the High Street, was laid out and numerous houses quickly constructed.[12]

Another area of recent development was the Brook, which stood between the High Street and Smithfield Bank. According to Hasted:

> It consists of a long row of houses, which have of late been greatly increased with streets leading from them up the hill, about the middle of which, at some distance from all others, is a number of houses, built closely together, called Slickett's Hill, so as to form a little town of itself. It is exceeding populous, owing to its numerous connections with the several departments of government, and the shipping business carried on at it.[13]

Immediately beyond these areas of new construction lay the daunting edifice of the parish workhouse. Standing at the far end of the High Street, this was also in the process of undergoing massive change. Originally constructed in 1725, it had recently been overwhelmed by the town's continuing expansion and the consequent increase in the numbers to be admitted. If nothing else, the workhouse now required to be considerably enlarged. For those who regularly attended meetings of the parish vestry, the problem seemed quite overwhelming. In fact, it was well beyond their limited capacities, bearing in mind that the vestry was entirely responsible for every area of parish administration. In searching for a solution, the recent success of the Commissioners who had taken responsibility for paving, lighting and cleansing of the High Street area must have been called to mind. It was decided that a separate board, to be known as the Board of Guardians, should be created and to be elected annually by members of the vestry and given entire responsibility for the needs of the destitute within the parish. This new board was sanctioned by Act of Parliament in 1802, and the first task undertaken was a general enlargement of the workhouse, so providing space for an additional 80 inmates of all classes.

Further radical changes to the administration of the workhouse were to take place in 1834. By that time, poverty having become an increasingly pressing issue, the government determined on far-reaching changes that would affect every parish in the land. Instead of individual parishes being responsible for the needs of the poor living within the community, a scheme was developed that called

61 Upon construction of New Road, funded through the levelling of tolls on those who used it, space was created for new housing. Among the first of an impressive collection of buildings that was eventually to line the road was Gibraltar Place. The central pediment reveals its construction date as 1794.

for the amalgamation of various parish authorities into combined groups that were to be known as Unions. Established under an Act of Parliament of 1834, this resulted in the parish of Chatham combining with those of Rochester and Gillingham to form the newly created Medway Union. A major requirement placed on the new authority was to make greater use of the workhouse concept, acquiring where possible much larger buildings that would cater for the combined needs of the several amalgamated parishes. Within the Medway Union, although such a move was eventually adopted, it was initially decided to make more efficient use of the existing workhouses within the area. Instead of the parish poor being sent to their nearest workhouse, now only females were to occupy the workhouse at Chatham. Destitute children living in Chatham and the rest of the Medway Union were sent to the workhouse of

62 In 1812, Gibraltar Place was extended. All dwellings were built over a high basement and given ornate mini-porticoes.

63 The houses which make up the 1812 extension to Gibraltar Place.

St Nicholas's (Rochester), while able-bodied males went to St Margaret's (Rochester). The Medway Union could find no use for the Gillingham workhouse because of its small size, and this was sold.

Away from the High Street, Chatham was appreciably less crowded. To the south, along New Road, there existed a more select residential sector. An extremely wide thoroughfare, New Road had been built to ease traffic congestion through the High Street. Additionally, it provided land for housing developments. Here, in 1794, was built the impressive Gibraltar Terrace, a series of three-storey, red-brick terraced houses that stand to this day. This became, together with Ordnance Terrace, the residence of the town's middle class. To ensure that traffic passed speedily along this road, its one potential bottleneck was completely removed: this was the point where New Road crossed Rome Lane (now Railway Street). A viaduct was built here, its foundation stone laid on 17 August 1779. Of red brick, and quite massive in construction, it carried New Road over Rome Lane, while the bridge it formed served as a military gateway into the town of Chatham.

In fact, New Road generally was an area to which the military had turned its attention when planning an extension to the Lines. In 1779, an Act of Parliament had empowered the purchase of an entire stretch of land between Chatham Hill and Rochester's Star Hill. This measure effectively prevented any further southward expansion of Chatham town. It also saw the destruction of some existing properties. With this latest military acquisition, Chatham was slowly hemmed in. To the west was Rochester, to the north the Cumberland Lines, and to the south land purchased by the 1779 Act and destined to become part of the Fort Pitt project that was to be completed in 1817.

Only to the east was there any possibility of outward expansion, this having taken place throughout the 18th century. The poor rate books trace the development of the 'County' or 'East Borough' of Chatham Town. In 1715 it comprised a mere 123 properties, but by 1726 it had reached 288. After this date the rate of expansion diminished, the number of properties in 1761 reaching 327. Even by 1801, though, housing in this area had not reached the village of Luton—something that was not to happen until the mid-19th century. The failure to build more rapidly

64 Constructed between 1819 and 1821, St John's Church was substantially altered and improved in the 1860s.

65 A general view along Rome Lane (now Military Road). St John's Church and the military gate (carrying New Road) can be seen at the far end of the street.

66 Clover Street's Zion Baptist chapel. Completed in 1821, it stood on a site long used by the Baptist community of Chatham.

67 Part of an engraving by John Cleverley Junior dating from the late 8th century. Entitled 'A View of Lewton near Chatham', it shows the rustic nature of the community with its unmade roads and quiet secluded cottages.

68 As Luton developed, it acquired a number of churches and chapels. Seen here is the Salem Chapel located in Crittenden's Meadow. (Les Collins)

69 Christ Church, Luton. Constructed in 1843 but demolished in the 1970s, it was superseded by a second Christ Church in 1884. (Les Collins)

to the east results partly from the nature of Chatham's industrial base, situated entirely to the west and based on the River Medway. Few employees wished to live this distance from their place of work. A number of chapels and a new parish church were built to meet the religious needs of those who lived in this area. Among the chapels was the Zion Baptist Church (Clover Street, 1821) while a new parish church, St John's, was built in Rome Lane close to the viaduct. Construction of the new church, which was to cost £17,000, began in 1819, and the building

was consecrated by the Bishop of Rochester during the autumn of 1821. Considered by many to resemble a factory building or assembly room rather than a house of God, it was one of the least successful church buildings to be constructed anywhere in the Medway Towns. Even more unfortunate was its lack of seating for the poor, the church catering primarily for the needs of the richer middle class. Eventually, however, its poor architectural style and limited concern for the less well-off were to be resolved, with a fundamental redesign and improvement during the 1860s.

Seven

A Town of Disease and Squalor

At Sly-Kate's Hill, ague, fever and small-pox with every disease peculiar to the town, are always to be met with, and the place is never without fever of the typhoid type.

Report to the General Board of Health on the Sanitary Conditions of Chatham (1854)

… I soon found Chatham was a bad place for a young single man. Too many temptations and enticements, that if you were inclined to keep yourself out of bad company it was a difficult matter to get into good company in such a place as Chatham.

Colour-Sergeant George Calladine (*c*.1837)[1]

The summer of 1832 saw the town of Chatham again in the midst of a crisis. A new danger had emerged and one much more deadly than those earlier fires. This time the threat was Asiatic Cholera, a feared disease that had a very low survival rate. During the earlier months of that year the disease had been ravaging northern England and London, and it was considered only a matter of time before cholera reached the crowded township of Chatham—a conurbation seemingly ripe for its spread.

Indeed, those responsible for administering Chatham had seriously failed to protect the health of those who lived there. Perhaps the worst feature was the large number of open sewers that emptied into one of the most important sources of local drinking water, the River Medway. Of these, Middle Ditch was of particular concern. Running along the back of the High Street, and completely open for about a third of a mile, it not only carried the effluent of numerous household sewers, but took away the filth of the High Street and waste from a number of slaughter houses. Similar ditches also ran the length of Military Road and Globe Lane. An even greater health hazard was a drainage ditch covered only by the wooden floor boarding of houses in Full-A-Love Alley. Those who occupied these houses were consequently living only seven inches above this fetid and foul smelling stream. If ever the floor boards were taken up, and they had to be frequently replaced because of dampness, they found themselves gazing upon a slowly flowing stream of inky black water.

Another of the town's health hazards was the waste that built up in the side streets. While the High Street, together with the wealthier areas of the town, was swept regularly, this was not so in the poorer residential areas. The result was that some roads, especially Rhode Street, Red Lion Alley and Horse Yard, were infamous for the accumulation of dung, manure, offal, filth and refuse.

The combination of open sewers and filthy streets ensured that Chatham was never free of some form of raging fever. Most common were smallpox and typhoid, while there could have been few who did not suffer gastric illnesses on a more or less regular basis. Most at risk were the newborn, with only one in seven babies surviving their first year of life. This gave Chatham one of the highest mortality rates in the country. Life expectancy was a clear six years lower than the healthier surrounding areas of rural Kent.

Given the poor state of hygiene that existed in Chatham, it is of little surprise that disease should suddenly descend upon the town. Making its arrival during the summer of 1832, it was eventually to claim more than three hundred lives. Normally entering the body by way of the mouth, cholera was usually contracted through consumption of food or water that had been contaminated by excreta of a cholera victim. Alternatively, it could be spread by flies that had either fed or

70 The temporary hospital for cholera victims was established in this building which lies adjacent to the covered slips in the dockyard.

hatched upon diseased excrement. The bacteria could last up to five days in meat, milk or cheese and as long as two weeks in apples or water. In beer, on the other hand, it could survive for only eight hours.[2]

Cholera first appeared on board the hulked warship *Cumberland*, a vessel that lay in the Medway and had been converted into a prison ship for the housing of convicts employed on building works in the dockyard. As soon as it was known that a number of them had come down with cholera, all convicts imprisoned upon hulks were immediately returned to them and not allowed ashore for any reason. With three hundred prisoners herded together, both day and night, on board the overcrowded and airless lower decks of *Cumberland*, the disease quickly took its

toll. Within a few days, over eighty convicts were reported sick, most of them failing to recover. A further victim was the surgeon of the ordinary, the man who attended these hapless victims. He died on 19 June.

In isolating the convicts, it had been optimistically believed that the disease would be kept out of the town of Chatham. Such hopes were quickly dispelled. On 17 June, the dock-yard surgeon was called to the home of William Dadd, a rigger employed in the ordinary. He recognised immediately the tell-tale symptoms of the feared disease, Dadd having lost large amounts of body fluid through violent vomiting and diarrhoea. This severe dehydration had caused widespread internal damage that led to a collapse of the circulatory system. Soon, the victim would take on a ghost-like appearance with the eyes sinking back into the sockets, nails turning blue, the skin livid and covered in cold sweat. By the time the surgeon arrived there was little that could be done to save William Dadd. All that was possible was an easing of the agonising muscular cramps that were a further feature of the initial dehydration. In desperation, however, the surgeon attempted to restore Dadd's circulation through the use of hot blankets. But, in reality, the unfortunate surgeon had not the slightest notion as to how his patient might be saved. In a mere six hours, William Dadd had been turned from a healthy and active member of the dockyard work force into a living corpse. On the day that followed the surgeon's arrival at William Dadd's house, cholera had claimed one further victim. In a desperate attempt to stop the disease spreading, all of Dadd's clothes and bedding were burnt. It was of little avail.

Another of the early Chatham victims was Quarter-Master Sergeant Hunt of the Royal Marines. According to the *Rochester Gazette*, he 'was seized by the disease while on parade'.[3] Although having the benefit of being taken into Melville Hospital—recently completed for the Navy and situated opposite the dockyard main gate—Sergeant Hunt was no more fortunate than William Dadd. Within hours of contracting the disease, he too was dead. Others in the Royal Marine barracks were demonstrating the symptoms of cholera, and several dozen were eventually buried on ground close to the hospital and well away from the petrified town dwellers, who knew not where the disease would strike next.

71 A view of the hulks of the River Medway. It was on board the crowded lower decks that cholera first gained a foothold.

The number of cholera victims mounted. Those who lived in the areas of Rhode Street, the Brook, Full-A-Love Alley and Slickett's (Sly-Kate's) Hill were the hardest hit. A number of hulks were converted into isolation hospitals, including *Scarborough* and *Warrior*. A cholera hospital was established within the dockyard itself, a temporary room situated over the pump house and formerly used as an iron store. At the time it was considered ideal, the room kept dry by the heat of the boiler, but such hospitals were useless. Together with the burning of clothes and blankets, they were a reflection of the mistaken belief that cholera was a contagion; it was not. It was spread by way of the open sewers, filthy streets and contaminated water supply. In these areas the authorities of the town should have concerned themselves.

At the beginning of July, there was a sudden upsurge in the number of victims. Many of them appear to have contracted the disease from the same source, having eaten sea food taken from the Medway. Those responsible for selling this food had been ordered out of town, the lobsters they were selling apparently being recognised as contaminated. After leaving the town, however, they stripped the claws from the lobsters and threw the bodies away. Returning to Chatham, they proceeded to sell the claws and it was of these that the new round of cholera victims had apparently partaken.

This event highlighted the difficulties that confronted those responsible for the health of the town. In essence, those who were in authority had no authority. At this point in time, neither the elected vestry nor Board of Guardians could confiscate food or arrest the sellers of food that was not obviously contaminated. After all, no one really knew how cholera was spread. In 1832, the nature of cholera was a highly contentious issue, with its pathological and clinical history yet to be understood. Apart from the vestry and

72 Although Melville Naval Hospital has long since been demolished, a few signs of its existence (including this brick wall) are still to be found among the flats that make up modern-day Melville Court.

guardians, one other body also now existed—a temporary Board of Health created during the previous year for the purpose of protecting Chatham against cholera. However, it had no real authority, being restricted to distributing precautionary and admonitory circulars. At Chatham, even this body was soon to be struck down, a victim of lethargy.

It was the subsequent winter that rescued the town from the grip of disease, the lower temperatures preventing its further spread. The arrival of a cold spell, though, had not always prevented the spread of such disorders. During an earlier winter period, that of 1813-14, a serious outbreak of typhus had continued unabated. On that occasion, the disease had broken out on board the Medway prison hulks but was entirely contained there, spreading only among those who were held on board. The difference was that typhus is spread by lice, these finding it impossible to survive outside the excessive overcrowding that existed on the hulks. According to Dr. William Burnett, who became senior Naval Medical Officer on the River Medway in March 1814, the continuing rampant fever was 'of a most malignant nature' and 'scarcely second to the plague itself'.[4] Those on board the hulks at this time were not civilian convicts but French, Danish and United States prisoners-of-war.

On taking up his appointment, Burnett immediately set about combating the winter epidemic. He showed great determination and later submitted a report to the Admiralty that is an amazing testimonial to this one particular doctor. It tells of his many colleagues that

succumbed to the fever but also shows how Burnett himself chose to ignore all risk, entering the hulks on a daily basis for the purpose of seeking out those who most needed his attention:

> ... he not only visited the infected ships daily, but was obliged personally for hours to be in their crowded and unventilated decks, selecting such men as were attacked to send them to the hospital. And so hazardous was this part of his duty considered that the officers of the most sickly ship attempted to dissuade him from it ...[5]

The use of the term 'hospital' in the above context is rather misleading. There was no permanent building serving such a role; Burnett was simply referring to another of the hulks that had been converted. In fact, Burnett had a number of vessels that had been set aside for the reception of those taken sick, among them *Crown Prince*, used by American prisoners, while the Danes were sent to *Defiance* and the French to *Trusty*. All of them had once been first-class fighting ships, *Crown Prince* having been captured from the Danes in 1807. As hospital ships, however, all three were ridiculously overcrowded and could serve no greater purpose than that of simply isolating the most serious cases.

Prior to Burnett's arrival, it appears that those brought to these vessels were considered to have little chance of survival. For this reason, most of the suffering prisoners seem to have been simply ignored and allowed to lie in their own filth. How else can the following addition to Burnett's report be explained? According to the good doctor, on his arrival at Chatham, he 'found in the hospital ship fifteen with their lower extremities more or less in a state of gangrene and almost every patient covered with patches of vibicis [bed sores]'. Only a lack of proper nursing could create such a situation![6] Not surprisingly, the survival rate was extremely low. Of those Danes and Americans who contracted the illness before Burnett's appointment, some 28 per cent died. However, following his arrival and insistence upon proper nursing, the survival rate jumped to a miraculous 89 per cent.

In the years that followed his service on the Medway, Burnett successfully climbed the ladder of promotion. In 1822 he was invited to join the Navy's Victualling Board (then also responsible for naval medical matters), which was followed by his later appointment to the post of Physician-

General. During these years he made frequent return visits to Chatham, regularly reporting on the state of medical care that was offered to those who either served in the Navy or were employed in the dockyard. One particular achievement was his insistence upon the need for a permanent hospital at Chatham, which came to fruition in the form of the Melville Naval Hospital. This building, the one that unsuccessfully treated Marine Sergeant Hunt, had sufficient room for 200 patients. The plans drawn up for its construction in 1825 showed that it was to consist of five separate buildings all linked by a covered pavilion. Three of these buildings were the wards (each of three storeys) while interspersed between were the dispensary and victualling room.[7]

Melville may have been the first purpose-built naval hospital in Chatham, but it was not the first to have been planned. At the beginning of the 18th century, Dr. William Lower, physician to William and Mary, had been commanded to put the medical affairs of the Navy into a more regular order. Working closely with Richard Gibson, a clerk at the Admiralty, he had proposed the construction of several naval hospitals to be built at Carisbrooke, Greenwich and Chatham. The latter was to involve the use of Hill House, a building then under-utilised by the Navy. However, despite the considerable value of such undertakings, only the hospital at Greenwich was finally established. The Army too had need for a hospital at Chatham, and the Ordnance Board oversaw construction of a building during the 1780s. Located on the Lines, it had a total of 12 wards and was able to accommodate 336 men.

Although the 1832 cholera outbreak in Chatham had shocked the local populace, nothing was done to remove the various health hazards that had so aided its rapid spread. Only the return of cholera in 1848 finally ensured that the terrible conditions existing in Chatham (and many other industrial towns) should be finally removed. By this time, the town had seen the establishment of a more powerful local board of health, with authority over drainage, sewerage and water supply. Unlike its predecessor, it was eventually to become a permanent feature of the town, reporting to the General Board of Health that had been established in London. An important undertaking by the new health authority was a report on the condition of Chatham which was published in 1852. Undertaken by William

73 Melville ceased to be a naval hospital at the beginning of the 20th century and was then passed over to the Marines as an extension to the barracks. Upon the departure of the Marines, it became a sight for a high rise residential flats.

Ranger, a superintending inspector of the national board, in conjunction with Dr. George Ely, surgeon of the Union Workhouse, it highlighted the constant prevalence of disease in the town and the dangers of the open sewers and unswept streets. Among recommendations made in the report were the removal of these sewers and their replacement by tubular drains, the effective cleaning of footways and roads using jets of water, and the introduction of an uncontaminated water supply based on water drawn from the Boxley Abbey spring. Following the setting up of a locally elected board of health, the recommendations of the report became major objectives that, once achieved, brought a remarkable improvement to the overall health of the town.

Another fundamental change to the town of Chatham was the achievement of Parliamentary Borough status. In the months that led up to the legislation that sanctioned creation of new constituencies and a wider franchise in 1832, those who lived in the town added their keen support. A number of meetings were held, of which the largest saw over 4,000 people in attendance. Held on vacant ground at the end of Military Road, a number of speakers called upon the King to continue supporting the proposed legislation while thanking Prime Minister Earl Grey for his advocacy of the bill.[8]

Among the leading organisers of the campaign in Chatham was a close relative of William Dadd, the man who contracted cholera during the same month that the Great Reform Act received parliamentary assent. This was Robert Dadd, owner of a chemist's shop in the High Street and an original member of the Chatham and Rochester Literary and Philosophical Institute that was founded at Chatham in 1827. At the crowded meeting held at the end of Military Road, Robert Dadd seconded a vote of thanks to those members of the two Houses of Parliament who were supporting the bill. Earlier, in May 1831, he had been a steward at a fund-raising dinner held by the Chatham branch of the Friends of Reform.[9] Chatham celebrated the passing of the Reform Bill by illuminating the town and raising a subscription to provide a celebratory dinner for the poor. The affairs of the Chatham Friends of Reform Committee had been wound up, Robert Dadd, who was its secretary, being described as 'indefatigable in his duty' and 'his labours immense'.[10]

As a result of the Great Reform Act, Chatham was able to elect its own Member of Parliament. Prior to that only neighbouring Rochester had possessed such a right, although a few residents of Chatham had cast their votes in either the city elections or within the wider county constituency of West Kent. The first election for the new Chatham constituency was held in December 1832, with the government candidate, William Maberley, receiving 363 votes as opposed to the 248 cast for his opponent, T.E. Perry. In accordance with laid down procedure, voting was by a show of hands (the secret ballot was not introduced until 1872), and everyone's vote was individually noted and subsequently published in a poll-book. Not surprisingly, corruption and vote buying was a frequent occurrence, although the election of Maberley was a reflection of the town's desire to elect those who supported the popular Whig coalition led by Earl Grey.

Another important Chatham reformer was the Chartist leader William Cuffay. He does not appear to have been politically active in Chatham but joined the Chartist movement in London.[11] In 1842 he was elected president of its Metropolitan Delegate Council, and he was an organiser of a mass meeting on Kennington Common held in 1848. On this occasion a petition containing two million signatures was to be presented to the House of Commons. However, on the day of the demonstration, Cuffay fell out with the executive committee and may well have supported more militant action. According to police spies, who frequently exaggerated the evidence they presented, Cuffay was one of several who plotted to fire certain buildings. At an Old Bailey trial, he pleaded not guilty and objected to the middle-class jury. Nevertheless, he was found guilty and sentenced to transportation to Tasmania which he reached in November 1849. Going back to his earlier years in Chatham, William Cuffay appears in the records of St Mary's Church as having been baptised on 6 July 1788. His parents were Julianna and Chatham Cuffay, their marriage having been solemnised at the same church a few years earlier.

William Cuffay was of Afro-Caribbean descent, his father having been born on the island of St Kitts. Almost certainly he was a slave, and would have been employed on one of the island's sugar plantations. How he came to the town of Chatham is something of a mystery, although it may have been the result of his having sneaked on board a naval warship and volunteered for service. This would have given him automatic freedom. Cuffay's first recorded appearance in Chatham is in October 1779, when he was mustered on board a sheer hulk in the River Medway. Such vessels, which were employed by the dockyard, were designed for the stepping of masts into warships, the sheer being a huge crane that was mounted on board the hulk. The name of this particular hulk, not inappropriately, was *Chatham*, and this doubtless was the origin of Cuffay's rather unusual first name. His son, William Cuffay, became an apprentice tailor before his move to London, and died in Tasmania in March, having received a free pardon in May 1856.

A number of other important changes were also witnessed by the residents of Chatham during the middle years of the 19th century. Among them was the introduction of gas (1827), a new enlarged cemetery (1828) which is now the Town Hall Gardens,[12] the Luton waterworks, which pumped clean water from underground wells and then piped it into Chatham (1856), the opening of Chatham railway station (1858), the first issue of a Chatham-based newspaper (*Chatham News*, 1859), the erection of a third parish church (St Paul's, 1854) together with a number of chapels,[13] the restoration and slight enlargement of St John's (1868)[14] and the founding of a volunteer fire service (1866).

Other changes were of a less beneficial nature. In particular, there was the new workhouse regime that followed the establishment of the Medway Union in 1834. In essence, it was designed to punish the poor for being poor. There was a belief that many able-bodied were deliberately avoiding work—even in times of high unemployment. Those entering the workhouse were, therefore, provided with a harsh and uncomfortable standard of living that involved unremitting labour broken only by sleep and a spartan diet of bread, cheese and wet pudding.[15] To further emphasise their detachment from the outside world, not only were inmates rarely permitted to leave the workhouse, but families were separated, with husbands, wives and children kept forcibly apart. Only on Sundays were families allowed to be re-united.

Although conditions in the Medway Union workhouse at Chatham were not as harsh as elsewhere, this did not prevent the local Board of Guardians from becoming embroiled in a number of embarrassing scandals. The first of these was in May 1842 and concerned use of a lodging house.

74 The original entrance to the new burial ground which was acquired by the parish in 1828.

Standing next to the Chatham workhouse, it was rented by the Guardians and was used to house vagrants and other temporary paupers. Little thought had been given to its proper management and a pauper was actually left in charge of the building. It further appeared that men, women and children were thrown together indiscriminately, sometimes with more than fifty paupers

75 Above the entrance to the new parish burial ground is a memorial stone recording that the land was acquired from the Board of Ordnance.

76 The year 1857 saw completion of the water pumping station at Luton. This Worthington Simpson beam engine was installed in the main pumping station. It remained in use until the 1950s. (Southern Water Authority)

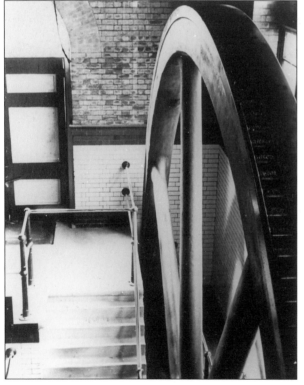

77 The 30ft fly wheel belonging to the Worthington Simpson beam engine. (Southern Water Authority)

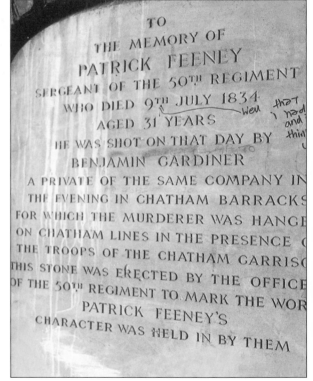

TO
THE MEMORY OF
PATRICK FEENEY
SERGEANT OF THE 50TH REGIMENT
WHO DIED 9TH JULY 1834
AGED 31 YEARS
HE WAS SHOT ON THAT DAY BY
BENJAMIN GARDINER
A PRIVATE OF THE SAME COMPANY IN
THE EVENING IN CHATHAM BARRACKS
FOR WHICH THE MURDERER WAS HANGE
ON CHATHAM LINES IN THE PRESENCE (
THE TROOPS OF THE CHATHAM GARRISO
THIS STONE WAS ERECTED BY THE OFFICE
OF THE 50TH REGIMENT TO MARK THE WOR
PATRICK FEENEY'S
CHARACTER WAS HELD IN BY THEM

78 A record of Chatham's more violent past. Recording the death of Patrick Feeney, the stone is in the new burial ground at Chatham. Given that it provides an interesting clue to a historic tragedy, might not greater efforts be made to protect it from vandals?

79   A general view of the Ordnance wharf that clearly shows the eclectic character of the parish church.

housed in a building that should have contained fewer than forty. During one period of six weeks, a soldier's wife, whose husband had been sent to India, was forced to suffer these conditions 'with a child at her breast'. During that time she was restricted to a diet of bread, cheese and water. Fortunately, friends of this woman came to her aid, helping her to supplement this diet with a more wholesome selection of foods.[16]

Following that particular scandal, it was revealed in January 1844 that the Guardians were supplying the Army with boys as young as twelve. Taken to the local barracks, they were encouraged to sign on as drummer boys. Their period of enlistment was always 'unlimited', resulting in their having signed away their lives at a time when they were far too young to give realistic consideration to their future.[17] At that time, even an apprentice at the age of 21 had the right to choose an alternative trade.

Finally, in June 1848, it was revealed that even the most deserving of the poor might find extreme difficulty in entering the workhouse

(or attached infirmary) if they arrived after 9 p.m. At that time of the evening, the knocker on the door was removed and the Master was reluctant to allow further admissions. Attention was drawn to this terrible situation by a member of the Chatham parish Board of Guardians, a body that had originally been formed in 1802 to oversee the Chatham parish workhouse. It had not disappeared in 1834 but continued the duty of collecting the poor rate within the parish of Chatham while also disbursing funds from a number of charitable donations. The poor of Chatham would sometimes present themselves to the parish guardians, as happened in June 1848. On that occasion, one of the guardians, M'Carthy Stephenson, brought to the workhouse for entry into the infirmary a destitute woman who was nursing a child with whooping cough. The time of arrival was a quarter-past-midnight, and both the child 'and mother completely saturated with rain'. It took over an hour for the door to be opened, a situation that drew not a mite of sympathy from the Medway Board of

80 A well-known Chatham landmark is the statue of Thomas F. Waghorn. Although born in Rochester, he enlisted in the navy at Chatham, becoming a midshipman in 1812. His claim to fame is not as a naval officer, but the development of the first practical overland route to India.

81 All Saints' Hospital. This section is part of the original union workhouse, established in Magpie Hall Road during the mid-19th century.

Guardians when it was drawn to their attention.[18]

Indeed, by that date the Guardians of Chatham parish, together with the vestry, had become watchdog bodies, determined to ensure that the poor of Chatham should receive better treatment. In April 1849, the two bodies combined, unleashing a particularly stinging criticism upon the Medway Guardians when they accused that board of misappropriating funds. The attack was led by Stephenson, a local solicitor, and it was indicated that too much money was being paid to the Clerk of the Board, a Mr. Buchannan, his annual salary having been increased by 100 per cent. Furthermore, during time in which he should have been working for the Medway Union, he was earning additional sums of money by illegally practising as a solicitor. Compounding all this was the Board's willingness to pay Buchannan's defence costs when his illegal activities were challenged by the Kent Law Society. To carry out further investigation into this and other matters, the vestry formed a special committee that demanded to examine the Medway Union's account books. This they had every right to do, being responsible for monies collected within the parish of Chatham. Gaining access to these books was of little avail for they had been very badly kept. In particular, huge amounts of money had been paid out, simply listed as 'sundries'. In a final report that was printed by the vestry after the raising of a subscription, the illegal defraying of Buchannan's expenses, together with the appalling state of the accounts, was highlighted and thoroughly condemned.[19]

A very different controversy was confronted by the Guardians of the Medway Union in 1856. This concerned a decision to build, at an estimated cost of £12,000, an entirely new workhouse on a recently purchased site alongside Magpie Hall Lane (later renamed Magpie Hall Road). This new building would be much larger than the original, so allowing for the closure of all three remaining workhouses within the Medway Union. Although construction of such a building made long-term economic sense, it did not meet with the full approval of Chatham ratepayers; they would need to meet the initial expense, something they clearly wished to avoid. A deputation from the various parishes was received by the Guardians in January 1857, the reason for a new workhouse was seriously questioned, and it was suggested that the present Chatham building might be further enlarged.

The Guardians remained unmoved, however, believing that any enlargement of the existing houses would be an extravagant waste of money. Three months later, the Board had approved plans for the new building drawn up by the Birmingham company of Peck and Stephens. As published in the trade paper, *The Builder*, these plans show that the new Chatham workhouse was to consist of one main building that housed separate wards for men, women and infants, together with staff accommodation and a dining hall. In addition, the site also included several out-houses used as isolation wards, accommodation for vagrants and a separate kitchen and boiler house. Tenders for its construction were received later in the year, and a local firm, James George Naylor of Rochester, was appointed builder. Among those employed to help in its construction were some workhouse inmates, most of them given the task of labouring and carrying.

It was completed in the autumn of 1859, and the Board of Guardians was able to order the transference of all inmates to the new building on 23 November. This allowed for the immediate disposal of the older buildings, and the Chatham workhouse and surrounding land was sold in various lots for the sum of £3,609. The building eventually came into the hands of the Axe Brand Machine Sewing Company. They installed 88 sewing machines and eventually employed 600 workers, most of whom were women.

The inhabitants of Chatham were affected by a new law enacted by parliament in 1864. Known as the Contagious Diseases Act (with amendments in 1866 and 1869), it was restricted to seaport and garrison towns and was ostensibly aimed at reducing the incidence of venereal disease among servicemen. At that time, the town had over 4,000 soldiers living within its boundary, and the incidence of venereal disease was among the highest in the country. The means of regulating it, however, was directed entirely towards the female prostitute rather than the male customer. Under the terms of the various acts, women might be compulsorily examined and, if found to be diseased, detained for up to three months.[20] Initially, this detention was in a special ward located within the recently built St Bartholomew's

82 The officers' quarters of the Marine Barracks in Dock Road. This building was completed in 1867 but demolished in the early 1960s.

Hospital in Rochester, but later a new building was constructed alongside Chatham's Maidstone Road within which only prostitutes were detained.[21]

That the middle period of the 19th century should see so much new legislation directed at the poor was the result of newly emerging middle-class fears. Such concerns were initially stimulated by the cholera epidemic of 1832, when the more affluent members of society became increasingly aware of how the poverty of the lower classes was spreading disease across society. This led to a desire on the part of the middle class to protect its own interests either by eliminating poverty or by forcing the poor to adopt different attitudes. Two methods were utilised: the expenditure of money on directly improving the worst aspects of town life together with a harshness towards the poor, which would encourage them to become more responsible. This latter policy was based however, on a sufficiency of employment. In Chatham, therefore, such a scheme could only have limited success. Between 1815 and 1840 the naval dockyard and ordnance wharf saw the loss of 2,000 jobs, while the victualling yard was permanently closed. No new large-scale employers arrived in the area, so the poor had fewer opportunities to work. In such a situation, how could they improve themselves? However harsh the regime, jobs were still required for them to earn the money to pull themselves out of poverty.

Eight

Incorporation

Chatham is a very different style of place to Rochester; a dirty unpleasant town devoted to the interests of soldiers, sailors and marines.

Handbook to the County of Kent (1876)[1]

While the health of those who lived in Chatham gradually improved, other aspects of town life remained singularly unchanged. In particular, much of mid-19th-century Chatham was characterised by a lawlessness reminiscent of Dodge City. In 1868, an enraged reader of the *Chatham Observer* chose to bring attention to the situation, hitting out at both the number of prostitutes in the town and the frequency of drunken fights in the High Street. He was concerned at the 'filthy vile language' of the former and their presence on 'every corner of our streets'. His main thrust, though, was directed towards 'drunken worthless soldiers out all night' who, according to the writer, were responsible for the constant outbursts of violence.[2]

In fact, the writer of this letter had little to complain about compared with the downturn of events witnessed during the 1880s. By then, the frequent fights had turned into large-scale riots. Often these were associated with naval ships returning to or leaving port. In October 1882, some 100 seamen from the warships *Constance* and *Linnet*, vessels about to sail for the Pacific and China respectively, marched four abreast along the High Street. Led by their own marshals, they stopped at various pubs, including the *Cross Keys*, where they demanded drinks but refused to pay. On leaving each of the houses, they were quickly assembled into parade order and boisterously continued their journeyings. The *Chatham Observer* anxiously reported the affair, pointing out that 'respectable people were roughly used and knocked about'.[3]

The divide between the 'respectable' folk and the 'roughs' of the town, terms frequently used by the local press, was particularly prominent in the reporting of such riots. In November 1881,

a crowd of 300 had gathered for the purpose of preventing the arrest of Robert Merritt, a coal whipper, accused of assaulting 'a respectable looking woman'.[4] Eventually, it took five members of the local constabulary to take him into custody, with the crowd going on to attack the police station in New Road. That matters did not get further out of hand was due to the timely arrival of a detachment of military police from the local barracks.[5] Two weeks earlier, on Guy Fawkes night, even more extensive riots had taken place on the High Street when a mob of over 600 assembled between Globe Lane and Military Road. On that occasion fireworks were thrown about indiscriminately and the streets were not cleared until after midnight.[6]

That such violence and general law breaking should be so commonplace in Chatham was a direct result of the town's lack of organised authority. This contrasted sharply with neighbouring Rochester, by comparison a haven of peace and tranquillity. Here, the elected Corporation was in a position to create its own police force and controlled the use of this body to enforce community legislation. In particular, the Corporation had considerable success in restricting pub opening hours, three pubs losing their licences in 1873 and a further five changing their ways as a result of police threats. Prostitutes rarely strayed beyond the limits of the parish of Chatham, knowing that if they entered Rochester their activities would be curtailed by the city police.

It was not a lack of policing but more a matter of resourcing and policy. Whereas the Corporation of Rochester had direct control of those who patrolled its streets, this was not the case with Chatham. Instead, the town was dependent upon a countywide force controlled by a Chief Constable. As a result, the numbers employed were relatively small, Chatham being allowed one police inspector and 12 constables for a population that had reached 26,184 by 1871, while Rochester had a Chief Constable and 28 constables for a population of 12,806. Not surprisingly, the efforts of those appointed to police the streets of Chatham were hindered by a simple lack of manpower.[7] Chatham was offered an increase in county police attached to the town, but leading ratepayers rejected the idea when they learnt that it would result in an increase in chargeable rates. They wanted more police, with the cost to be shared equally by the entire county. Not until 1885 were they granted this wish, when the Chatham and Gillingham division received a dramatic 30 per cent increase in the number of officers allocated to the area.

The improvement was the result of efforts by three leading members of the community: George Church, Adam Stigant and George Winch. George Church was the influential owner of 'The Royal Emporium', a large draper's store that stood on the site of present-day Marks and Spencers. A leading member of the local Liberal Party, he had been elected to both the Board of Health and Medway Union. George Winch, on the other hand, was a Conservative. For much of this period he was clerk to the local Board of Health, although he resigned this post in March 1889. In addition, he was clerk to the stipendiary magistrates at Chatham, local returning officer and a county alderman. A fairly affluent member of the community, owner of Holcombe, a large house in Maidstone Road which now provides accommodation for Chatham Grammar School, he had donated a sizeable sum of money to St Bartholomew's Hospital for the building of a new wing.[8] Adam Stigant, who sat on a number of local committees including the Joint Hospital Board and the Medway Board of Guardians, also chaired the local Board of Health. Politically, Stigant was probably the most influential of these individuals, his chairing of the Board of Health placing him in a position to negotiate directly with the mandarins of Whitehall. Brian Joyce notes that contemporaries of Stigant regarded him as 'the uncrowned King of Chatham': 'Without him the situation here would seem pretty much akin to a performance of *Hamlet* with the part of the illustrious Dane left out.'[9]

The three men appear to have come together during the mid-1880s, agreeing that Chatham would greatly benefit from a Charter of Incorporation. This would allow for the establishment of a powerful elected body that could oversee much of the future development of the town. Initially, they looked for incorporation with Rochester and Gillingham, this allowed under the Municipal Corporations Act of 1882, which permitted any incorporated borough with a population of 50,000 to take on the greatly extended powers of a county council.[10] However, both Rochester and Gillingham rejected this possibility, anxious to avoid domination by the much more sizeable population of Chatham parish. Had such an amalgamation taken place, it would have created one of the most powerful municipal authorities in the country. Pre-dating more recent local government changes, it would have allowed the Medway region to create its own integrated transport system, an educational structure worthy of a forward-looking town, and a much needed municipal theatre together with other entertainment venues.

Following rejection by Rochester and Gillingham, a meeting of Chatham ratepayers was held on 25 August 1888, which unanimously agreed to apply for a Charter of Incorporation. This would allow for the establishment of a properly constituted town council. While not having the power of a county council, it would bring under one authority a variety of separate bodies that had been established over the years. In particular, the newly elected councillors for the town would take responsibility for education, health and sanitation as well as acquire influence over the number of police appointed to the town.

It was at this point that George Winch came to the forefront of the campaign. He was appointed solicitor on behalf of the campaigning committee, eloquently presenting the case for incorporation at an enquiry held before the Local Government Board inspector. According to the *Observer*, 'Mr. Winch marshalled his facts and his figures in such a masterly style that it was then generally believed that the petition would be granted.'[11] Although it was as a result of George Winch's efforts that the Charter was granted, those in Chatham were surprised by the length of time taken to reach a decision. The new borough was not officially gazetted until 22 November 1890.

83 A pen and ink sketch from the *Chatham and Rochester Observer* depicting the reading of the new borough charter.

George Church,

THE DRAPER,
ROYAL EMPORIUM,

HIGH STREET,

CHATHAM.

———•———

SEASONABLE
           DRESS FABRICS.

NOVELTIES IN
           LACE GOODS.

SOFT KNITTED
           UNDERWEAR.

LATEST STYLES IN
           MILLINERY.

NEW AND DAINTY FURS.

FASHIONABLE JACKETS.

RELIABLE FAMILY
           DRAPERY.

84 One of the leading campaigners for Chatham's borough status was local trader George Church, owner of the Royal Emporium. Situated at 154 High Street, the Emporium ceased to trade in 1934, when it was taken over by Marks and Spencer.

The Charter itself was delivered into the hands of George Winch, provisionally nominated first Mayor of Chatham, on 10 December 1890. Together with Adam Stigant and several other Chatham notables, he had been called to the Home Office for this purpose. Taking possession of the document, they returned to Victoria station where a larger deputation had assembled. Everyone had been brought to London by a saloon carriage laid on by the London, Chatham & Dover Railway Company. All now returned to Chatham in this same carriage where they were met by a huge crowd that lined the route along which the new charter was to be paraded. The procession, which was led by the band of the First Kent Artillery Volunteers and included all children attending local schools, wound its way along Railway Street and New Road before entering Luton Road and Castle Street. Eventually the procession turned on itself, walking the length of the High Street. Its objective was the Board of Health offices, which were at the top of Military Road. Here speeches were made prior to the reading of the Charter by Frederick A. Stigant, the provisional town clerk.[12] Unfortunately, the day itself was marred by much unruly behaviour, some of those assembled outside the Board of Health offices attempting to enter the building. In doing so they nearly brought down a temporary stand upon which the local M.P., Sir John Gorst, and other guests were seated. The police, as on so many other occasions, seemed quite powerless, so proving the need for an empowered body to oversee the future direction of the town.

The establishment of a town council was to transform Chatham. With greater powers over the expenditure of money, important initiatives were soon embarked upon. Among the most notable was a road widening scheme in the High Street (1898), the purchase and laying out of Victoria Gardens (1897), Town Hall Gardens (1905) and the Paddock, while a public weighbridge was sited at the end of Globe Lane.[13] However, the most expensive single project was the building of the Town Hall, undertaken between 1898 and 1900. Providing offices for the different municipal departments as well as a council chamber, it replaced the small and cramped Local Board of Health offices that served the needs of the council during its first nine years of existence.

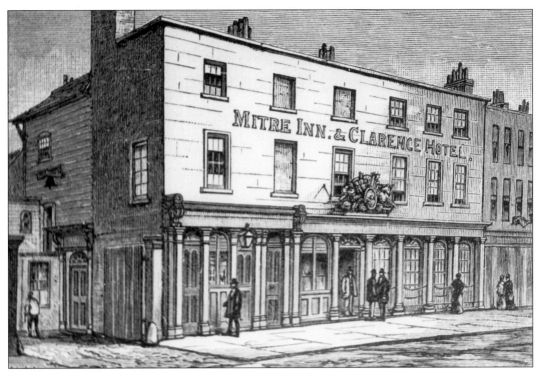

85 *The Mitre* began life as a coaching house and was, supposedly, frequented by both Lord Nelson and the future King William IV. It was one of the many drinking venues that once dominated the centre of Chatham.

More important, from the point of view of bringing about a greater degree of orderliness to the town, was the influence the new council exerted upon the county-controlled police. More officers were attached to Chatham and they were directed towards the effective enforcement of licensing laws. One of the most notorious pubs in Chatham, the *King's Head* in the Brook, appeared to harbour most of the town's criminal fraternity. Aware of this, the council not only revoked its drinks licence but proceeded to oversee the transformation of the building into a temperance café.

The Brook was, in fact, at the very heart of Chatham's problems. In this and other nearby roads were the numerous pubs that housed most of the town's prostitutes. Destroy this area, it was assumed, and the majority of the town's problems would disappear. One approach was the steady removal of older buildings, the council acquiring a portion of the Brook for the building of the Town Hall and the construction of new houses. Within a few years of Incorporation, one of the worst streets in this area, Full-A-Love Alley, was completely obliterated, replaced by the newer

and wider Batchelor Street which opened out into the High Street.

In its task of improving Chatham, the council received much needed assistance from various religious bodies. Certainly, some new places of worship were built during this period, including Christchurch (1884) and St Andrew's Presbyterian Church (1903). At the same time, extensive rebuilding and restoration of St Mary's parish church (1884-1903) and St Bartholomew's Chapel (1896) was also undertaken. The 18th-century exterior of the parish church was completely formed into its present-day mock-Gothic appearance, while St Bartholomew's Chapel was restored and given a reconstructed nave and additional north aisle. Much more important, though, were attempts at countering the temptations of drink that confronted the local soldiers and sailors. A Royal Navy mission was established in the Brook, providing classes, meetings and entertainment of a religious, social and educational character. Should the 'blue jackets' not appreciate this, there were rest homes. These were designed as an alternative to the pubs

86 At the east end of the High Street is *The British Queen*, a pub with a quite exquisite tiled entrance that betrays its Victorian origins.

87 A rare view of Chatham High Street with one of its many notorious pubs on the corner of Military Road. This site has long been occupied by Burtons.

and brothels, having a pub atmosphere minus the alcohol. Both the Methodist Church and Salvation Army ran such homes, and they provided sleeping accommodation, billiard games, reading rooms and canteens.[14]

Other aspects of Chatham life were under improvement during the latter years of the 19th century. The west end of the High Street, in particular, saw the establishment of several music halls and a theatre. The earliest dates back to 1846 when Dan Barnard established his 'Palace of Varieties', which ran in conjunction with a small pub, the *Railway Tavern*. Barnard was actually an important contributor to the well-being of

Chatham, being a founder member of the local fire service. Following his death in 1879, the 'Palace of Varieties', which may well have been the earliest variety theatre in the country, was destroyed by fire. The new proprietor, Lou Barnard, one of Dan's many sons, decided that another theatre should be built, this one considerably bigger and better than the original. Opened in July 1886, and known as 'Barnard's New Palace of Varieties', this second music hall dispensed with the idea of a separate pub, having two bars incorporated into the design.

A further Barnard family project was the Theatre Royal, a more up-market venue intended for the performance of popular plays. Opened on 31 July 1899, it was built at a cost of £30,000 and had seating for approximately 3,000. On its first night each of these seats might have been sold six times over, suggesting that the theatre was well on the road to financial success. Unfortunately, and rather ironically for a family so closely associated with the town fire service, the theatre succumbed to an unaccountable blaze only 10 months after its opening. Despite the hurried arrival of both military and civil fire-fighting parties, the entire stage and much of the auditorium was gutted. It was not until December 1900 that the Theatre Royal was again in a position to receive the public.

88 Numerous attempts were made to 'clean up' the central Chatham area, with the establishment of numerous temperance institutions such as the Welcome Sailors and Soldiers Home in Military Road, designed to attract servicemen away from the consumption of alcohol.

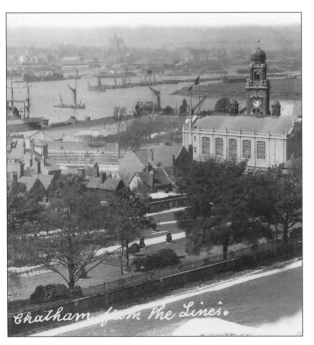

89 Chatham from the Lines. A general view of the newly incorporated town of Chatham.

90 The local barracks were not entirely without forms of entertainment. This colonnading in Dock Road is part of the original entrance to the Soldiers' Institute and Garrison Club. Completed in 1861, it was run by a joint military and civilian committee with facilities that included smoking and coffee rooms, a bar, library and bowling alley.

One further theatre established at the west end of the High Street was the Gaiety, opened in June 1890. This was also a music hall, but appealed to a slightly higher class audience. The new theatre not only had three bars, situated on the ground floor, dress circle and gallery, but a retiring room where tea and coffee were served. The original owner of the Gaiety was entertainment proprietor Mr. J. Chaney of Gravesend, who financed most of the building costs, said to be in excess of £6,000, together with a further £9,000 for fixtures and fittings. Constructed on the site of a former hotel, *The Imperial*, part of whose façade was utilised, the theatre itself stretched further back, some 156ft., almost to the River Medway. Seating capacity was in the region of 1,000, with 450 of these in stalls, the most select area. Here, for instance, where prices were at their highest, arm chairs were supplied, which were far more comfortable than the benches found elsewhere.

91 The rebuilding of St Mary's Church included the construction of an entirely new bell tower. Named after Queen Victoria, it was dedicated in February 1898.

93 One of several new churches built during this period was the Luton Road Bible Christian Chapel. This building was demolished during the 1980s. (Les Collins)

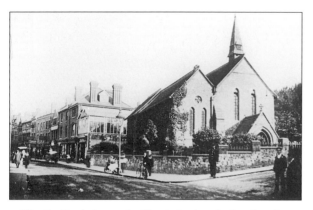

92 St Bartholomew's Hospital chapel shortly after completion of restoration work that had been overseen by George Scott.

94 Christchurch, Luton. Constructed in 1884, it replaced the earlier church (of 1843) that had stood on the site. (Les Collins)

95 Chatham Town Hall stands in the midst of the Brook. Completed in January 1900, it now serves as an art centre and theatre.

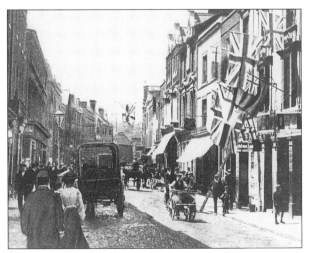

96 Chatham High Street, *c.*1900. The flag-bedecked building to the right is The Empire, one of two music halls that provided Chatham with regular entertainment.

97 An alternative to the music hall was The Theatre Royal, with a programme of visiting repertory companies. At the time of writing, considerable efforts are underway to restore the theatre to its former glory.

Also undergoing considerable change during this period was the dockyard. A significant turning point had been the laying down of the iron battleship, *Achilles*, in 1863. This was the first major warship of metal construction to be launched in any of the government yards, marking Chatham out as the lead yard for all future ships of this type. Following the building of *Achilles*, there was a massive extension of the dockyard, which absorbed St Mary's Island and effectively quadrupled the yard in size. Built primarily by convict labour, the centrepiece of the new extension was three huge basins built along the line of St Mary's Creek. They allowed warships to be brought into the dockyard for fitting and refitting, such work having previously been undertaken while ships were moored in the river. The extension also included numerous docks, various

98 The Chatham 'Empire', the second of Chatham's music halls.

99 A government plan to bring about a massive expansion to the dockyard was discussed in the 1820s. Eventually sanctioned in the 1860s, it was to add 380 acres to the existing yard. Here, work is underway upon three massive basins that ran the length of St Mary's Creek.

100 Much of the work on the dockyard extension, which took it into the parish of Gillingham, was undertaken by convict labour. Here, a number of convicts are being escorted to their work on St Mary's Island.

ploying a total workforce of 4,199. This represented a 140 per cent increase over the equivalent figure in 1860.

Much of the dockyard extension works crossed the boundaries into Gillingham, but the influence on the town of Chatham was still considerable. Many of the newly recruited workers continued to live in Chatham, placing increasing pressures upon those responsible for administering the area. Of particular concern was the fact that many of the newly employed workers were not entered on to the establishment (as permanent members of the workforce) but were only given hired status and could be dismissed at any time. The concern of those who lived in Chatham was that many were being attracted to the area but might, at any point, become a burden on the town. In 1887, for instance, over 1,000 dockyard workers were dismissed, the result of a sudden change in government policy and of the yard's need to economise. Many workers were able to leave the town, returning to their original homes, but others had settled permanently. The result was another local crisis, with hundreds of families throwing themselves upon the Guardians of the workhouse. For once, the elected Guardians began to show real sympathy for those they protected, even agreeing to give out-relief to those they might normally have brought into the workhouse. Following a request from a woman who sought assistance for herself and her children while her husband looked for work elsewhere, they decided there was little real alternative. 'We are

factory buildings, a pumping station and hydraulic cranes. By 1883, with final completion of the extension, the dockyard at Chatham was em-

101 While building of the massive extension proceeded, the Chatham end of the yard found itself fully absorbed in building new iron-clad warships. The vessel under construction in No.2 Dock is probably *Hercules*, launched in 1868. The large building to the right was the first to be erected in a royal dockyard for the construction of iron ships.

sure to have a number of cases of this kind,' stated the chairman whose words were reported by the *Chatham Observer*. 'I am sure the members will not wish to smash the homes up.'[15]

A further important issue was the lowness of the dockyard wage, this especially affecting the hired men who did not have the benefit of job security nor a future pension. Unlike workers in many other industries, it was these men, primarily unskilled labourers, who led the resulting protest movement, forming themselves into unions and acquiring the support of local Liberals (including Arthur Otway, M.P. for Chatham, 1865-74). The campaigning zeal of the unskilled industrial workers of Chatham dockyard peaked on two separate occasions, 1872 and 1891. In both years, pay rises were granted which not only benefited the unskilled hired workers. In order to maintain the differential pay scheme, the Admiralty also increased the wages of all classes of worker employed at Chatham, as well as those in other naval dockyards. The leaders of the unskilled workers were James Kingsland and William Lewington.[16] The former was elected secretary of the Society of Dockyard Labourers in 1872 and was instrumental in acquiring the support of Arthur Otway. William Lewington, who at one

102 Turn-of-the-century Luton was still seen as a rural environment where those living in Chatham town could find the peacefulness of the countryside.

time lived in a small cottage near Little Crown Yard, was founder of the Chatham Dockyard Labourers' Protection League and led the campaign of 1891. This second pay increase, the direct result of Lewington's work, led to his being the beneficiary of a public subscription that awarded him a black marble clock, a purse of gold and an illuminated framed address. Among those who contributed were not only the workers of the

103 This early 20th-century photograph of Luton village centre shows that housing was beginning to creep into every available space. (Les Collins)

Liberal-Conservative committee was established for the purpose of arranging free entertainment for a number of Chatham-based soldiers recently posted to the war zone. This was the 2nd Battalion of the Royal Lancashire Fusiliers, stationed at Chatham barracks. The entertainment was two smoking concerts held on consecutive nights at the Gladstone Hall (Liberal owned) and the Queen's Hall of the Constitutional Club (Conservative owned), both of which were in Military Road.

The Relief of Ladysmith (February 1900) resulted in the raising of flags on all public buildings, the ringing of church bells and a half-day holiday for schoolchildren. However, it was the Relief of Mafeking (May 1900), news of which reached Chatham on Friday the 18th, that really caught local attention, with the High Street and Military Road becoming the scene of spontaneous rejoicing. Patriotic songs were sung and an immense crowd released its pent-up feelings by repeated outbursts of cheering. By Saturday morning decorations had sprung up everywhere and during the evening there were illuminations and the Band of the Volunteer Rifles performed an open-air concert.

Both Barnard's and the Gaiety produced a number of patriotic sketches that reflected events in South Africa. As early as the second week of the war Barnard's included the sketch 'For the Honour of the Regiment'. As the war had become unexpectedly drawn out, many of the performed sketches later became little more than overt propaganda. 'The Boer and Britain', staged in March 1900, centred around enemy misuse of the white flag.

The Gaiety had an advantage over Barnard's in that, prior to the war, it had installed a Scot's 'Metascope' which projected animated pictures on the stage. In December 1899 audiences were treated to films that showed early skirmishes outside Ladysmith and the embarkation of Sir Redvers Buller for South Africa. A picture of President Kruger was hissed, while his departure from the Transvaal parliament was accompanied by the 'Dead March' in *Saul*. Following the showing of these films, the Frances Harold company presented 'Under Which Flag?', involving the wreck of an armoured train and a fight with the Boers.

The return of individual troopers and their regiments fostered further street celebrations. In

yard but many tradesmen in the area, the latter emphasising that his efforts had benefited the whole area by increasing 'the wealth coming into Chatham'.[17]

Rounding off the century for Chatham were various events associated with the nation's involvement in the South African or Boer War (1899-1902). Throughout most of the period of hostilities, there was little local opposition to the war, a bi-partisan approach having been adopted by the Chatham branches of the two main political parties. Even the general election of 1900—known as the 'khaki' election—was a non-event, with the Conservative, Horatio Davies, returned unopposed.[18] At the outbreak of the war, a joint

104 A scheme pioneered by George Winch, one of the campaigners for Chatham's borough status, was the creation of a free public library. To speed things along, he donated £250 towards books and a building. A site was located at the east end of New Road and the newly formed council agreed to go ahead with construction. It was eventually opened in October 1903, the first appointed borough librarian being Mr. E.E. Buddery.

105 The predecessor of Chatham's first free library was the Mechanics Institute. This building stood in the High Street and was originally established in 1837 'for the promotion of useful knowledge among the working classes'. It ran a regular programme of lectures and operated a lending library for members.

June 1901, James Presnail, a future alderman of the borough and author of a history of the town published by the borough council in 1952, was invalided home, having contracted enteric fever. Although the cause of his return was unassociated with the fighting, he was still treated as a hero. Welcomed at the railway station by members of the local rowing club (of which Presnail was a member) and the Band of the Volunteer Rifles, he was carried shoulder-high to a waiting carriage, and ceremoniously escorted home. The rest of Presnail's regiment, the locally recruited West Kent Company of the Imperial Yeomanry, returned on 19 July. Arriving at Strood station, they were met by the Band of the Royal Engineers and escorted in marching order to the Town Hall at Chatham. A huge crowd once again assembled along the entire length of the route.

The proclamation of peace in 1902 was a further cause of mass celebration. News that the treaty had been signed reached Chatham on the evening of 1 June, and crowds soon gathered outside the Town Hall. Everywhere congratulations were offered, while evening church services included special prayers. On the following day, decorations were again visible along the main thoroughfares, while those arrested during the previous night's celebration received an unconditional pardon when they were brought before the bench.

Nine

Into the Twentieth Century

The other day a sharp boy moving along the Brook shouted out 'Hurrah for Jenkins' and someone—who he supposed came from the Constitutional Club in Military Road—called out 'Hurrah for the Devil'. To this the boy replied, 'You shout for your man and I'll shout for mine'.

Chatham News, 13 January 1906
[Report on the election of John Jenkins, Chatham's first Labour Member of Parliament]

As the borough of Chatham entered the 20th century, the town was on the verge of a transport revolution. A tramway system was under construction that would soon stretch to every corner of the borough. Fifty cars provided a cheap and rapid service that would give a journey time of less than fifteen minutes from Luton village to the dockyard.

There was considerable enthusiasm for the scheme, and the Chatham and District Light Railways Company was inaugurated in October 1897.[1] A comprehensive plan had been proposed, designed to stretch the line through Rochester and into Strood. As with the earlier idea of a unified borough council, Rochester again resisted.

106 In order to allow trams ease of access into Chatham from the cemetery and Maidstone Road, it was necessary to build a new viaduct.

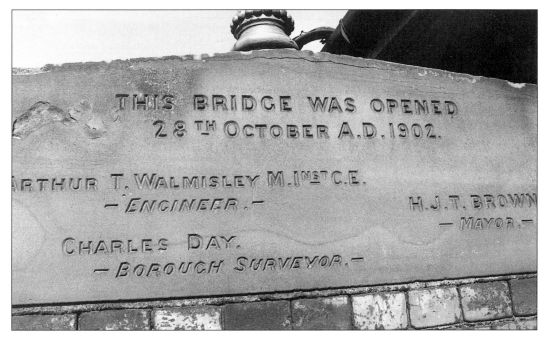

107 The commemorative stone placed on the viaduct (or bridge) recording its official opening in October 1902.

108 The starting point of the tramway system was the *Hen and Chickens*, Luton. This was a point close to the tram depot.

109 A tram bound for Chatham cemetery leaving the general interchange at the town hall. Instead of numbers, the trams were designated by letters, in this case C-B (Gillingham—Town Hall—cemetery).

Too many of its citizens were against such progress, so initial proposals were restricted to Gillingham and Chatham, with construction work beginning in March 1900. The most obvious features of the new system, the metal rails, overhead lines and supporting poles, were a fairly straightforward building task. The rails, which were supplied by the Barrow Haematite Steel Company and weighed nearly 100lb per yard, were to be laid in a concrete foundation that would provide an exceptionally smooth ride. All the electric equipment was supplied by the Thomson-Houston organisation, which had a controlling interest in the 'Chatham and District' Company.

More demanding, and ultimately more expensive, were a number of road widening schemes that accompanied the laying down of the rails. A Board of Trade enquiry held at Chatham in 1898 gave permission for the tramway system but identified a number of potential bottlenecks that would need attention. These had to be removed before any tram would be allowed to run. It was left to the council to undertake these works, the 'Chatham and District' agreeing to pay £7,500 towards the overall cost. Among these projects was the complete removal of the old defensive brick arch and gateway that stood across Railway Street. Originally built during the 18th century, it also served as a viaduct, with New Road running across the top. The necessity of its removal was less a matter of age and more a result of its narrowness, the entrance gateway preventing trams reaching the Town Hall from the direction of Maidstone Road. Because the archway also carried New Road its replacement needed to be of a wide span yet capable of carrying considerable amounts of traffic. The outcome was the present-day girder bridge, officially opened on 28 October 1902. Unfortunately for the 'Chatham & District', the cost far exceeded an original construction estimate cost of £1,500; the company was required to pay an additional £5,500.

Another important requirement was the construction of a tram depot and power station. These were both situated in the village of Luton about 200 yards short of the tramway terminus at the *Hen and Chickens*. The power station, which generated current for the entire system, was equipped with three compound engines and five boilers built by Yates and Thom of Blackburn. Immediately alongside stood the main tram depot. This had space for about sixty cars, stored one behind the other on eight separate lines. In addition, the depot contained inspection bays and full workshop facilities for the maintenance of vehicles.

The Chatham tramway system, officially opened on 17 June 1902, was centred on the Town Hall. Every single route crossed at this point, providing a convenient interchange for passengers wishing to make an onward journey. In 1912, Edwin Harris, who produced an early guide to the new borough of Chatham, chose to describe the various routes that were then available. Each of these journeys had as its starting point the Town Hall:

> Route 1. To Gillingham Green and Church, and within easy distance of Lower Rainham Road, its orchards, quaint old cottages, and mansions on that highway.
>
> Route 2. To Jezreels and the *Shalder's Arms*, via Canterbury Street, passing Gillingham Park, and terminating near the Island Gate of H.M. Dockyard.
>
> Route 3. To Rainham, an old-world Kentish village and its Church. Magnificent views are obtained by the outside passengers, not only over the Luton Valley, but right down to the Nore; and even Southend is visible on a clear day.
>
> Route 4. To Chatham Cemetery on the Maidstone Road, and the Football Grounds. From the terminus a pleasant walk brings the pedestrian on to Blue Bell Hill, where unrivalled views of the Weald of Kent and Sussex can be obtained.
>
> Route 5. To the Pembroke Gate of H.M. Dockyard, Royal Naval Barracks, and other Government establishments.
>
> Route 6. To the *Hen and Chickens*, Luton, where a short stroll takes one to Darland and the Bredhurst Woods.
>
> Route 7. To Borstal, with splendid views of the Valley of the Medway, and Cobham Woods.
>
> Route 8. To Frindsbury, through the High Streets of Rochester and Strood. Leaving the terminus, a pleasant walk can be taken to the river-side villages of Upper and Lower Upnor, an ideal place for a day's picnic.
>
> Route 9. To the top of Strood Hill, within 20 minutes' walk of Gad's Hill, the residence of the late Charles Dickens, which is open to visitors by kind permission of the owner on Wednesdays only from 2.15 till 5pm.[2]

110 Another tram, this one bound for New Brompton (Gillingham), passes the old post office. This building, recently turned into a pub, appears to have disgorged many of its postal workers for the benefit of the camera.

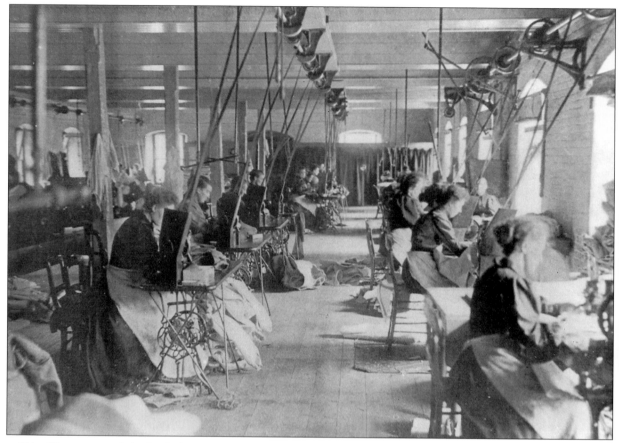

111 Women at work in the dockyard colour loft, *c*.1900. This, and the ropery, were among the few areas that saw the employment of women during this period.

Probably no route would have been busier than the one leading to the dockyard. Overnight, the yard 'mateys' had been given a fast and comfortable means of getting to work. As a result, the choice of where to live was greatly widened, especially as the tramway system began in Luton. Many new terraced houses were built here to meet the demand, ensuring that Luton became an important suburb now permanently connected to its much larger neighbour.

These dockyard-bound trams would occasionally find themselves carrying large crowds of people to witness the launch of new warships. Undoubtedly, the most important of these launches, following the turn of the century, was that of *Africa*. A 16,350-ton battleship, she was the last such vessel to be built at the yard, Chatham going on to specialise in submarine-building. That no more battleships were launched at Chatham had

much to do with the River Medway, considered too narrow to accommodate the new 'dreadnoughts' that would soon enter the Navy. At first, the future of the dockyard looked bleak; it had, after all, once been the lead yard in the construction of all large warships, and the wealth and prestige of the area was dependent upon such work. Yet Chatham did not really lose out. Between the launch of *Africa*, in May 1905, and the outbreak of the First World War, four cruisers, six dockyard tugs and a range of support vessels were built there. In addition, Chatham was the first government dockyard to build a submarine, the C.17, which was launched in August 1908, and went on to build a further 11 during the period prior to the war. On top of this, of course, there was a large amount of repair, fitting and refitting work which ensured that the yard was fully employed and that those who worked there received a secure wage.

112 Launch of *Africa*, the last battleship built at the dockyard.

113 *Africa* proceeds along the Medway to join the Atlantic fleet.

A Mass Meeting

IN THE

TOWN HALL

On SATURDAY, December 3rd.

Frank Smith, L.C.C.,

THE LABOUR CANDIDATE,

SUPPORTED BY

J. KEIR HARDIE, M.P.,

WILL ADDRESS THE MEETING.

Chair to be taken at **8.**   All Electors Welcome.

A. W. IRELAND, Election Agent.

114 Despite Labour's convincing victory of 1906, the party failed to retain the seat in 1910. The unsuccessful Labour candidate in December 1910 was Frank Smith.

DEARER FOOD

WITH THE RADICALS IN POWER.

It was **the Radicals** who told you at the last General Election, when they wanted your votes, that your food would cost you more if the Unionists were returned.

It was **the Radicals** who promised you the "Big Loaf" if you gave them your Votes.

Consequently, the Radicals were returned to power. What followed?—Cheaper food?—Easier Living?

NO !

Dearer Food and a heavier weekly budget for the poor man's family.

	Under the Radicals	
Your Coal cost more		Your Tapioca cost more
Your Tea cost more		Your Raisins cost more
Your Bacon cost more		Your Sultanas cost more
Your Soap cost more		Your Kitchen Utensils cost more
Your Cheese cost more		Your Cotton Goods cost more
Your Cocoa cost more		Your Linen Goods cost more

YOUR FOOD COST YOU MORE UNDER THE RADICAL FOOD-TAXERS.

VOTE FOR HOHLER THIS TIME

and tax the Foreigner.

115 The successful Conservative candidate in 1910 was Gerald Hohler. He retained the seat until 1918.

Another important talking point for those who used the Chatham tramway was the election of the borough's first Labour Member of Parliament. In January 1906, John H. Jenkins of the Labour Representative Council defeated the Conservative candidate, Major J.E. Jamieson, by a majority of 2,672. This was an incredible turnaround for the borough, the people of Chatham having been represented by a Conservative member for the previous 32 years. Furthermore, Jenkins was only to hold the seat for four years, being defeated in 1910 by Gerald Hohler. That Chatham should be one of the few constituencies to return a Labour member during this particular general election is the result of a deal between the Liberal Party and Labour Representative Committee, by which the two organisations agreed not to compete. At Chatham, the failure of the Liberals to take the seat since 1874 had led to its being offered to Labour. It was felt that the new party might appeal more to dockyard workers, many of them voting Conservative in the belief that the Liberals favoured building warships in private yards.

For many of those who lived in Chatham, John Jenkins' greatest appeal was his being a shipwright.

He was not a local man, however, having been a former mayor of Cardiff and a prominent worker for the Labour cause in that city. His election campaign emphasised his affinity with the workers of the yard and Jenkins promised that he would attempt to bring parity of wages to the private and government yards. The Conservative candidate stressed his party's recent spell in government, during which time the dockyard wage bill had peaked at

116 New Road as it was shortly after the turn of the century.

£14,000 per week. He claimed that a Liberal government would reduce this to £4,500.

The days leading up to the poll were characterised by a series of massive party meetings at which late-comers struggled to find even standing space within the enclosed confines of the selected venues. A Labour meeting at the Town Hall, held on 7 January, was so crowded, that an overflow meeting had to be held outside. A cornet player started the proceedings, accompanying the assembled audience with a song that was rapidly becoming the local Labour anthem, 'Goodbye Horatio'. Played to the tune of 'Blue Bell', it was a reference to Horatio Davies, the outgoing M.P. for Chatham. Even at Conservative meetings, which were ticket-only events and designed to keep the opposition outside, Labour supporters could still be heard singing this provocative little number.

Declaration of the poll was an eagerly awaited event, with hundreds assembled outside the Town Hall and along Military Road, the heartland of political Chatham. As the minutes ticked by, loud cheers for Jenkins would rent the air, with less resounding counter-cheers being heard for Jamieson:

> Exactly at twenty minutes to eleven the Mayor (Councillor H.F. Whyman), as returning officer, made the formal declaration of the poll from the balcony overlooking the Military-road. There was tremendous cheering at the mention of the name of Jenkins, and when Alderman Jenkins appeared on the balcony in sight of the crowd the cheering was vigorously renewed and maintained for several minutes. Meanwhile the poll was 'declared' upon an illuminated screen, as follows:-

BOROUGH OF CHATHAM

RESULT OF POLL

Jenkins	6692
Jamieson	4020
Majority	2672

The crowd went wild with excitement on seeing the startling figures, and loud cries of 'Good old Jenkins' were heard on every hand.[3]

John Jenkins was to prove an efficient and honest Member of Parliament who worked tirelessly for the dockyard and those it employed. During the four years he held Chatham, the borough grew markedly in prosperity, with the dockyard receiving frequent orders to carry out new building and repair work. Yet, at the general election held in January 1910, the Conservatives were able to win back the seat with a majority of 1,281. In part, this must be credited to a change in the constituency, with the Royal Navy Gunnery School moving to Chatham from Sheerness. This placed a great number of seamen onto the voting register, many of them swayed by the Conservative candidate, Gerald F. Hohler's emphasis on a strong Navy rather than a prosperous dockyard. In addition, a number of more moderate Liberals appear to have turned against Labour and withheld their vote. Indeed, during a second general election, held in December 1910, Labour fortunes plummeted even further when a Liberal candidate entered the contest. This effectively split the opposition vote, resulting in an increased Conservative majority.[4]

Away from transport and politics, the borough of Chatham was also being revolutionised in other areas. Moving pictures had arrived when the 'Cinema de Luxe' threw open its doors on 22 January 1910. This was Chatham's first picture house, a converted shop that stood at the west end of the High Street and advertising a continuous performance that lasted from 3pm until 6pm. The 'Cinema de Luxe' was noted for its cramped, uncomfortable wooden benches and, in its first year, a projected picture that constantly flickered. Even so a capacity audience was a frequent occurrence. Doubtless this was the case during the first week, when films shown included a drama entitled 'The Brothers', and a political comedy, 'Scroggins Puts up for Blankshire'. This last was of particular interest as it told the story of Scroggins, a candidate for parliament who was bombarded by members of the suffragette movement. Its showing at the 'Cinema de Luxe' also coincided with the first of the two general elections held in that year.[5]

Approximately a year later, on 15 April 1911, a second Chatham cinema was opened in the form of the 'National Electric Theatre'. Unlike the 'Cinema de Luxe', this was a specially designed building erected at a cost of £3,500. Able to accommodate an audience of 600, the 'National'

is supposed to have had some of the most up-to-date equipment of the day; unfortunately there were still a few teething problems on the opening night and complaints that films shown were out of focus. Seat prices varied from 3d. for an orchestra stall to 6d. for the balcony and stalls. The 'National Electric' showed films until 1950, when the building, which still remains, was converted into a shop.

Largest of the cinemas in those pre-war days was the Imperial Picture Palace, which opened in January 1914 and was usually known more simply as the 'IPP'. Standing at the east end of the High Street, it was a more luxurious venue than either of the others and had a total capacity of 1,700. Seating was of the newly invented tip-up kind, while two 'Simplex' projectors overcame the problem of flickering. Originally owned by the Chatham and District Cinema Ltd., the 'IPP' remained as such until August 1927. In that month, having fallen into the hands of a new lessee, it became 'The Regent'. In February 1930 it was taken over by Associated British Cinema, who between January 1937 and July 1938 carried out a full rebuilding programme.

The outbreak of war in August 1914 was an event that brought great prosperity to the area, but this was more than countered by the huge loss of life, with no Chatham family untouched. Among the first of a long list of tragedies to affect the town was the sinking of the cruiser *Pathfinder* on 5 September 1914. Torpedoed in the North Sea by the submarine U21, her crew had not only been mustered in Chatham, but many had families in the town.

A few weeks later, the loss of *Pathfinder* was to be completely overshadowed by a tragedy of enormous proportions. Early on the morning of 12 September, three Chatham-based cruisers were sunk, leading to the loss of 1,500 lives. The cruisers, *Hogue*, *Cressy* and *Aboukir*, were all torpedoed by U9 while on patrol in the North Sea. A rumour of this terrible event appears to have reached the town by about midday, when hundreds of distraught women gathered outside the town hall. At first, the authorities would say nothing, but eventually an official statement was posted, merely confirming the loss of the three vessels. With the Town Hall serving as the central recruiting office for the area, large numbers chose to remain outside, waiting for a list of survivors.

117   The Chatham 'Empire'. A new cinema was opened alongside this building in 1916.

118　In contrast with industrial Chatham was the continuing rural nature of Luton, where hop picking was to continue into the mid-20th century. This picture, probably dating from September 1906, shows members of the Phillips family at the end of a busy day. (The Phillips family)

Eventually, the full extent of the tragedy was revealed, and many had to accept that they would never see their loved ones again. Among them were two sisters-in-law, next-door neighbours, who learnt that their husbands, the Hussey brothers, Tom and Jim, were both dead. For James Goodrich, a Chatham greengrocer, there appeared to be better news. He had heard, unofficially, that his son, a leading stoker on *Aboukir*, had survived. Yet, on the list of survivors pasted to the wall of the town hall he could find no mention of his son's name. In order to confirm that he was alive, Goodrich made a special journey to Whitehall. On returning to Chatham, his daughter ran to greet him, anxious to learn of his news. She failed to check for traffic and to his grief, James Goodrich saw his daughter run down by a horse bus. In one week, the poor man lost two children, for the news he brought from Whitehall was that his son had drowned in the North Sea.[6]

Later in the war, the civilians of Chatham came under attack. On the evening of 17 September 1917, four German Gotha bombers carried out a raid upon the dockyard. None of the bombs hit the intended target but were spread across the Medway Towns. One fell on the High Street at Chatham, while another landed in the cemetery. Fortunately, neither of these caused any loss of life. However, another of the bombs, a 110-pounder, crashed onto the naval barracks, exploding within the drill hall then being used as sleeping quarters. In all, 136 naval ratings were killed, earning this one single bomb the gruesome record of causing more loss of life than any other dropped throughout the entire war.

Despite the sadness of war, the east end of Chatham High Street continued to serve as a focal point of entertainment. The music halls and Theatre Royal continued to do a roaring trade, with the 'Picture Palace' cinema (which adjoined the 'Empire') also opening its doors in February 1917. Among films shown on that first night, and reflecting the wartime concerns of the nation, was *Advance of the Tanks*. It showed this particular weapon in action, and is described by a local newspaper correspondent:

> The sight of the unwieldy looking monsters going into action, smashing like matchwood the German wire entanglements and other obstacles, was a thrilling spectacle, while the audience also obtained a good idea of what strafing the enemy lines is like.[7]

A few months before the opening of 'The Empire', the dockyard took on a 16-year-old electrical apprentice, Cyril Cate. Cyril's significance is the result of his enthusiasm for keeping a diary of passing events. Although his early diaries are sparse in detail, those he kept in later years are of great interest. He records not only personal items, but events going on around him. The earliest entries take place during this wartime period, with Cyril recording that during the summer of 1916 he successfully passed the Chatham Dockyard entry examination.

By entering the yard, Cyril was continuing a family tradition. Other members of the Cate family had been long there, his father, William, as a shipwright. More recently, in March 1916, Emily, his eldest sister, had entered the yard's torpedo department. Women were being encouraged to undertake such work for the purpose of releasing men into the Army. Cyril was too young, and was to pursue his dockyard apprenticeship for the next two years but, upon reaching the age of 18, he too joined the Army.

The war came to an end in November 1918, the occasion of considerable celebration within the town of Chatham. Mostly, this was of an unplanned nature, with many houses quickly displaying flags and colourful bunting to mark the event. Much more organised was the huge victory march that coincided with the signing of the official peace treaty in July 1919. This great occasion centred on the Town Hall where a saluting base was erected, occupied by Major-General Sir Herbert Mullaly, General Officer Commanding the Thames and Medway. At the head of the procession was the Band of the Royal Navy Barracks followed by a detachment of the Royal Navy with four field guns: 'These men were typical blue-jackets; fine stalwarts, hearty fellows, every one of them, and their appearance was a signal for hearty cheering.'[8] Other elements of the Navy included in the march were the Marines and Wrens, following close behind. The Wrens, in particular, were commented upon, the local newspaper describing them as 'looking very trim and smart'.[9] Every military body with a wartime association with Chatham was included in the march, the Royal Navy followed by the Royal Engineers, Royal Army Medical Corps, the Women's Army Auxiliary Corps, and the various infantry detachments that were then billeted in the town barracks.

Ten

And on to the New Millennium

As an industrial centre the Borough has many advantages—excellent communications by land and water, cheap motive power, abundant water supply, etc. The whole of the river frontage is now almost exclusively taken up with Government establishments and private wharves for corn, timber and other commodities.

Chatham Official Guide, 1927

The Armistice of November 1918 brought a sudden and not unexpected period of economic depression to the town of Chatham. Since the 1880s, the dockyard, together with other elements of local industry, had either been preparing for a war or actually fighting one. The dockyard, in particular, had gone through a long period of industrial expansion, with all of its slipways, docks, fitting and repair basins crowded with ships demanding attention. In 1885, the yard had employed a work force of 5,000, but this figure had doubled by 1903. By November 1918, the yard had peaked at a new figure of 18,000.

There was now a need to economise. First to go were those who had been recruited during the war. These were mainly men and women trained to undertake a few specialised tasks,

occupying positions now required by men returning from the front. This should have been good news for those who had left their jobs and volunteered to fight, and were expecting to get their old jobs back. Cyril Cate, for example, returned to the yard in 1919 and was allowed to continue his broken apprenticeship. Others, however, were often less successful and, upon returning from France, were only offered labouring jobs. Even if they turned to their union they were given little support, those representing the yardwork force far too weak to engage upon such issues with the Admiralty. In 1926, for instance, the dockyard unions were discouraged from giving any support to the General Strike and work proceeded as normal within the dockyard. Indeed, Chatham was used as a centre for

119 The launch of submarine X-1, 16 June 1923. One of the limited number of new ships launched at Chatham during the inter-war years.

strike breaking. Large amounts of coal, destined for various power stations, were constantly despatched by train. This was dockyard coal originally brought to the yard for powering ships and yard machinery.

Elsewhere in Chatham, there were pockets of support for the strike. In particular, local railway and tram workers gave it their full backing. However, it was still possible for the public to travel, a number of newly formed independent motor bus companies continuing to run as many services as they could during this period. Similarly, those responsible for printing the *Chatham News* and *Chatham Standard* remained at work, allowing these papers to report on the progress of the strike. The *Chatham News* proclaimed in an editorial that,

> the papers from this office will be continued as long as circumstances permit … In dealing with the crisis, it is our intention to adhere strictly to facts; to express no opinion as to the pros and cons of either side; and not to report rumour or hearsay, or reproduce inflammatory and alarmist matter likely to spread disaffection.[1]

While the majority of those living in Chatham remained fairly neutral towards the events then taking place, others actively volunteered their service as strike breakers. A recruitment centre was established in the town, and some 500 individuals offered their support by the end of the first week. While it is not clear as to how they were employed, many doubtless found themselves involved in the trans-shipment of food or the movement of railway engines.

A slightly different form of opposition also began to emerge, according to the *Chatham News*:

> A feature of the strike was the strong antipathy shown towards it by women. Many men called out by their unions experienced difficulties because of this. On being told by her husband that he had been ordered with the rest of the members of his trade union to cease work, one good local lady promptly declared: 'If you strike, I strike, and it'll be no use you coming home to meals, because I shan't get them for you!'[2]

Shortly after the General Strike, trams in Chatham ceased running completely because of increased competition from motor buses; trams lacked the speed, comfort and flexibility of the petrol-driven vehicle. Realising that there was

no future in the existing system, the 'Chatham and District' determined that it would cease operating trams on 30 September 1930. The company was not surrendering to the competition, though, merely re-entering the market place on its own terms. The following day, 1 October, the company's brand new fleet of 37 Leyland 'Titan' double-deck motor buses began operating along the former tram routes. Any competition had been effectively disarmed by a parliamentary act that allowed the company to transfer its operations to motor buses while giving the 'Chatham and District', now re-named the Chatham and District Traction Company, a local monopoly. In return, though, the company had to provide low fares for those travelling to work. To help facilitate this major change, work was put in hand to convert the Luton tram depot (which was to be completely rebuilt in 1970) for the accommodation of motor buses, the maintenance pits being filled in and petrol tanks installed. Over the next few months, many of the old tram lines were removed from the streets of Chatham, and eventually no visible sign remained of this noisy but once essential means of transport.

Another dramatic change to the centre of Chatham was the enforced demolition of Barnard's New Palace of Varieties, the building seriously damaged by fire in March 1934. On the night of the 18th, a discarded burning cigarette end appears to have gone unnoticed following the evening performance. With the building closed and in darkness, a fire soon took hold, remaining undetected until nearly midnight. At that point, a resident in nearby Medway Street woke to see flames leaping out of a rear window. Despite the arrival of three fire tenders and a host of firemen from Rochester, Chatham and Gillingham stations, nothing could be done to save the theatre. Instead, an all-out effort was made to protect surrounding buildings, with the main fire simply contained. By morning, therefore, the former variety palace was no more than a smouldering wreck, having clearly witnessed its last performance. Yet, if nothing else, its departure from the local scene had been truly spectacular, with huge 30ft. flames visible for distances in excess of six miles.

At that time, the whole concept of the music hall was in obvious decline. Almost certainly, Barnard's New Palace of Varieties would have been forced to close its doors, anyway, through a simple lack of audience. The fire, if anything,

120 Theatre programme.

seemed fortuitous, the building having been suitably insured. The rival Gaiety Theatre was certainly beginning to struggle, its proprietors forced to show films as a means of economic survival. This apparently worked, with the Gaiety soldiering on into the 1950s. A willingness to experiment appears to have been the key to its survival, even moving over to a continental style, with acts such as 'Les Jeune Filles' and 'Les Dillionaires' advertised in 1959.

The reason for this decline in the popularity of local music halls was the continued improvement and expansion of the cinema. During the 1920s, Chatham High Street could boast four separate dedicated film theatres, the 'National Electric', the 'IPP', 'Empire' and the 'Invicta'. The last, situated in Fullager's Alley and first opened in February 1916, was part of a local chain of cinemas owned by the Croneen family of Gillingham. The senior member, James Croneen, had been a dockyard employee before investing his skills in the building and renting of houses during the boom expansion years that occurred towards the end of the previous century. His other cinemas were in Gillingham and Strood.

However, the 'Invicta Picture Palace', together with the other Chatham cinemas, was soon overshadowed by further developments during the 1930s. In that decade, a whole host of new film theatres were opened, with the 'Palace Super Cinema', which was built at the top of Chatham Hill, the first to draw Chatham

121 Staff at Chatham's re-opened Regent cinema in 1938.

audiences. Within easy reach of both Chatham and Gillingham, it was, from the outset, part of the massive Gaumont-British enterprise. Eventually in 1950, renamed 'The Gaumont', a particular feature of this new cinema was a stage directly linked to the screen. This, it was hoped, would make it appear as if the action were performed on stage, so giving an 'intimacy between audience and actors which may be unique'.[3] At the opening on Monday 30 November, guest of honour was Anna Lee, known in the film world as 'Britain's Glamour Girl'. Aptly chosen, Anna Lee had spent much of her early life in the Medway Towns, deciding to enter films after seeing *Ben Hur* at one of the numerous Chatham cinemas. The 'Palace Super Cinema' continued to show films until 1961.

The second of Chatham's super cinemas was 'The Ritz', built on the site of the original parish workhouse and opened by Jack Buchanan in March 1937. Unfortunately, this particular building, which served more recently as a bingo hall, no longer survives: it was the casualty of a major fire in September 1998. Built by Union cinemas, the 'Ritz' was particularly luxurious, the furnishings carefully chosen to blend with its moulded ceilings, heavily piled carpets and ornamental mirrors. Sound reproduction, provided through the latest mirrorphonic system, was considered to be of a particularly high standard. The opening was another magnificent occasion, featuring a mix of film and live entertainment. On stage was Billy Cotton and his band together with the Dagenham Girl Pipers, while a special round of applause was reserved for Harold Ramsey, world-famous organist, who gave a highly polished performance on the cinema's giant Wurlitzer organ. The screened film, almost an anti-climax, was *My Man Godfrey*.

Last of Chatham's three super cinemas was the rebuilt IPP/Regent. It was taken over by the Associated British Cinema Company in February 1930, who oversaw its complete rebuilding and subsequent fitting out with the very latest sound and projection equipment. On its re-opening on 11 July 1938, the first films shown starred Otto Kruger in *Housemaster* and Dorothy Lamour in *Thrill of a Life Time*. The highest priced seats were 2s. (10p) while front stalls were 2d. and rear stalls 5d. Eventually renamed the ABC in 1970 (and later Canon), it has subsequently been converted into three separate screens that allow for the showing of a greater number of films.

122 The Ritz cinema building. Destroyed by fire in 1998, it had opened as a super-cinema in March 1937.

Returning, for a moment, to the diaries of Cyril Cate, he has much to say about the dockyard, which continued to be his place of work until his retirement in the 1960s. Launchings, in particular, are well recorded, with Cyril himself present on 16 March 1926 when a 'County' class cruiser first entered the River Medway:

> I went to No.8 Slip and saw launched successfully HMS *Kent* by Lady Stanhope. Public allowed and crowds of people ... attended. *Kent* in the North Lock (for purposes of entering the fitting-out basin) by 3.30 in the afternoon.

A large number of more general activities within the yard are also recorded in the diaries. In September 1926, he refers to the demolition of a dockyard hoist (known as 'sheer legs' because of its similarity to a pair of shears) that had once been used for the fitting of ships' engines:

> Sheer legs on No.2 Basin were demolished. They are forty years old and condemned as unsafe. All ships were cleared from basin and at 12.30 a charge fixed to lower part of back leg was exploded and the legs allowed to fall into the water.

He also gives a series of daily reports on the success of the second of the annual Navy Weeks which was held at the dockyard during the summer of 1929. The major attraction on this occasion, apart from the ships that were open to the public, was a display in one of the basins of a captured Arab gun-running dhow. On the first day, Monday 12 August, Cyril recorded in his

123 The Chatham Historic Dockyard Trust, which is now marketing the dockyard as 'The World Naval Base', has partly adopted a Second World War Two theme. Here, a pill box has been enhanced by additional pieces of armament.

diary, 'a good number of people to have been present'. On the following day he must have given the impression of being one of the exhibits on display. Helpfully reinforcing the public notion that yard workers rarely exerted themselves, he spent the entire day 'sitting on the foc'sle of [HMS] *Hawkins*'. For the rest of the week he continued to comment on the immense numbers visiting the various warships open to the public. On the Saturday, however, instead of entering the yard as a worker, he joined the general public and boarded a number of warships as a visitor.

The opening of the dockyard during Navy Weeks remained an annual event until 1938, the one planned for the following year being cancelled due to the likelihood of war. It was the greatest of all Chatham events, with numerous cruisers, destroyers and submarines open to the public. At the same time, demonstrations and displays were

taking place all round the yard, allowing the public to appreciate more fully the work of the Navy. As well as thousands of local residents, the event attracted visitors from throughout the south-east. To ease their passage into Chatham, railway and bus companies organised special excursion trips from London and other parts of Kent while paddle-steamers brought vast crowds from Southend and Sheerness. By 1938, the event was regularly attracting crowds in excess of 90,000, adults having to pay an entry fee of 1s. while children were admitted for 6d.

The town of Chatham continued to reflect the existence of a large military presence within its immediate geographical area. As well as the Royal Marine and Chatham Infantry barracks, both of which were in the town of Chatham, there were three additional military barracks within close walking distance. HMS Pembroke (naval barracks completed in 1903), St Mary's (an infantry barracks built in 1808) and Brompton barracks (the home of the Royal Engineers and completed in 1806), were all within the borough of Gillingham. Each housed hundreds of young men who, eager to break the monotony of the barrack block existence, frequently descended on the town, all looking for entertainment. This, in part, explains why there were so many music halls, cinemas, pubs and other recreational facilities within the central town area.

Although Chatham of the '20s and '30s was very different from the town that existed 50 years earlier, there was still considerable prostitution and occasional outbursts of violence. In particular, the Brook still harboured a fearsome reputation, with pubs such as the *Dover Castle*, *Army & Navy* and *Duke of Clarence*, fondly remembered by ratings and squaddies alike. In the High Street, the *United Services*, sometimes known as Mother Knott's, was famous for its western-style long bar and frequent fights. Yet, levels of violence should not be exaggerated. By now, there was considerable policing in the town, with the local constabulary ably supported by the military police and naval provosts.

The substantial military presence brought with it the regular spectacle of military parades and marching bands. Once a year, the Royal Engineers would pass through the town, the Corps marching to a special service at Rochester Cathedral. On other occasions, the comings and

124   Recently restored, and now on display, is this Second World War canteen.

goings of various infantry regiments belonging to Chatham barracks would draw a regular crowd. As for the Royal Marines, their departure was often through the dockyard, regular detachments marching to their assigned ship accompanied by the divisional band. Jack Lacey, who wrote an account of his time at the Royal Marine barracks, refers to these occasions:

> … all the squads of 'men standing out about' (a formal term) were called to attention and faced towards those who were about to embark upon their Imperial Duty. None could fail to be affected as the name of one of the five great naval stations was shouted in the command. 'HMS *Delhi* detachment—to China! Quick March!' and led by the Drum Major and the band the detachment marched out of the Ceremonial Gate towards the Royal Dockyard, past weeping wives and longing sweethearts.[4]

125   The mobile kitchen was a gift to the dockyard from Canada.

126   The centrepiece of a dockyard display opened in 1999 is HMS *Cavalier*, a Second World War destroyer that actually ended its naval career at Chatham.

Lacey, in fact, provides quite an insight into barrack life, describing such intimacies as the importance of the clock to all who served within the perimeters of the red-bricked Marine barracks. As he was repeatedly told, 'The BBC, the International Date Line, Greenwich Mean Time have no meaning here. All time is measured by the Barrack Clock. It is always right!' Elsewhere, he tells of barrack rooms holding 23 recruits sleeping upon paliasses of straw:

The Room Corporal and the trained-soldier had the privilege of foam mattresses which in retrospect did not have the same capacity for inducing sleep, but the privilege lay more in not having to change the straw once a quarter. The stables lay a quarter of a mile up the steep Brompton Hill. There was something of a treat about the task. The sight and smell of fresh straw, horses—known as hacks and chargers—and piles of manure beside what seemed then a great barn, where we tumbled and skylarked to fill a paliasse was a great break from the endless parade drill.[5]

Life in Chatham changed considerably as the result of the outbreak of war in 1939. The day before war was declared, some 2,000 children from the Chatham area were evacuated into rural Kent. The belief at the time was that Chatham would be subject to heavy aerial bombardment, with the nearby countryside that much safer. Already the town had been given some idea of what might lay ahead, a mock air raid in May 1938 seeing 18 aircraft from Manston supposedly destroying a number of key installations and an incendiary bomb narrowly missing the railway station. To help ensure that this did not become reality, Chatham was blacked-out at the very beginning of September, with Cyril Cate remarking on the 'complete black-out at night', adding that 'sandbags were everywhere, and that everything was 'looking warlike'. As for the dockyard, Cyril further added, '[4 September 1939] Maidstone and District buses in yard being converted to ambulances. Police patrolling sheds with metal helmets.'

Many of Cyril Cate's entries during the early months of the war refer to visits to Sellindge, to where his family had been evacuated, and the occasional difficulties he now encountered in getting to work. Things were particularly difficult during the early winter of 1940, the weather adding to the general gloom. On 29 January there was a heavy snowfall, Cyril declaring two days later that 'all buses stopped, roads too icy. Many chaps out from work'. Confirmation of these appalling weather conditions can be found in that week's *Chatham News*: 'This week's weather has been responsible for the worst traffic hold-ups experienced in the Medway district for many years.' The newspaper went on to confirm that buses had 'sometimes been unable to leave their depots', while at 'other times only a "skeleton" service had been in operation'. Adding to the problem was the fact that drivers of many lorries had been forced to abandon their vehicles on Chatham Hill.

Further problems in getting to work were encountered in February, when a visit to Chatham was made by King George VI. The visit itself was planned for Tuesday 21st, and the King was to visit the Royal Marine Barracks and the dockyard. On the Monday, the visit was announced in the form of a snap rehearsal. Many roads around the dockyard were closed, and Cyril himself was caught out as a result of leaving the dockyard for dinner and being unable to return along his normal route. On the following day all must have seemed worthwhile, Cyril getting a glimpse of the 'sailor king' as he passed 'through our hot room'.

It was the German invasion of Norway and Denmark in April 1940 that announced an end to the 'Phoney War' and the beginning of the real conflict. This was brought home to Cyril by the entry into the dockyard of a number of war-damaged ships. Among them were the destroyer *Hotspur* and the anti-aircraft cruiser *Curacoa*. Both vessels had been in the thick of an action fought in Narvik fjord, *Hotspur* colliding with another destroyer after coming under heavy fire that resulted in the loss of her steering. *Curacoa* had been repeatedly dive-bombed, receiving a direct hit between decks and losing 30 of her crew. Of the arrival of these two vessels at Chatham, Cyril noted, '[2 May 1940] Saw destroyer *Hotspur* come in badly peppered by shell fire at Narvik and her bows stove in. *Curacoa* also came in damaged by bombs'.

The Chatham area suffered its first air raid on 18 June 1940, the target probably the dockyard. Cyril records that he 'woke up suddenly at 11.30 by bomb explosion from German raid'. According to that week's *Chatham News*, it was one of the biggest air raids so far experienced, with Kent 'one of the eight counties visited by German bombers'.

A more intense series of raids followed in mid-August, when rarely a day was not disturbed by wailing sirens. Cyril Cate later calculated that the amount of time lost in the dockyard during August due to raid warnings totalled 20 hours. In an overnight raid on 28/29 August, the dockyard was severely pounded. Cyril was able to survey the damage:

> Came to work this morning. Saw much damage by bombs. Two large craters near our shop. One section had all overhead windows smashed. Had no electricity and gas. Work at a standstill mainly all morning. EHI [possibly Engine House] offices cleared of people. Back part demolished. Air raid warning for one hour at 3.50. Warning again at 6.20 to 7.25.

127 *Ocelot*, launched at Chatham in May 1962, has been returned to the yard for display purposes.

In mid–September, Cyril witnessed an aerial dog fight which took place over the yard:

[17 September 1940] Alarm went at 9.35. All clear 10.30. Saw British Hurricane come down on [St Mary's] Island. Pilot baled out. Warning went at 12.35 and had quite an exciting time watching about 12 large bombers and heaps of [enemy] fighters attacked by gun fire and our fighters. Saw machine come down and parts of a bomber. Some bombs dropped on Lower Gillingham … Saw great bodies of German bombers attacked by AA fire and turned back. Saw machines fall. Also our own Hurricanes. Large bomber fell in pieces over Upnor Hills.

The diary entries for the final quarter of 1940 continue to detail numerous raids and countless warnings that continue right up to the middle of December. On the night of 8/9 October, Cyril records a further raid on the dockyard, the damage visible to those who came into the yard on the following day. He notes in his diary the destroyer *Hambledon* lying 'in basin with her stern underwater'. That same day also brought a further raid on the dockyard and the immediate surrounding area: 'Siren went at 11.35pm and a number of planes passed over with heavy gunfire. Heard a bunch of bombs falling'. The dockyard, which continued to be a major target, was subject to several further raids during this period. On 25 October Cyril records that upon entering the yard in the morning he heard a couple of bombs 'whistle down': 'One fell on ambulance bus near dockyard garages. Wrecked SNSO [Naval Stores] offices [while other bombs fell] in Victorian shed in garden on island in dockyard and knocked out SNSO office near garage'. A more serious raid took place on the dockyard during the late evening of 3 December, when nine bombs fell on the factory and the No.5 dock riggers' workshop (close to the No.1 basin) and several members of the dockyard Home Guard were killed or badly injured. For Cyril, who was a member of this same Home Guard battalion, this was quite a shock. The funeral of those killed took place on 7 December: 'Funeral today at Chatham cemetery of Home Guards killed in Tuesday night raid on Dockyard. Dockyard HG [Home Guard] formed firing party'. The final raid of the year, according to Cyril's diary, took place on the night of 14 December.

> HM SUBMARINE OCELOT WAS THE LAST WARSHIP TO BE BUILT FOR THE ROYAL NAVY AT CHATHAM DOCKYARD

128 An inscription proudly emblazoned within the dockyard.

A warning was given at 6p.m. while he was still on his way home from work: 'On way heard Jerry plane flying low and dropping bombs all round. Dropped at Chatham. All clear at 7.50. Went round to Mr. Winchester [a family friend] and heard bombs dropped in the vicinity of Ordnance Street'. He goes on to note that there were many who were killed and injured while 300 were made homeless.

Although the dockyard and the town of Chatham were to be subjected to further raids, including an onslaught from flying bombs and V2 rockets, the extent and frequency was much reduced from December 1942 onwards. Furthermore, Cyril Cate, who so accurately recorded events during these years, left Chatham, having volunteered to serve with the Dockyard Mobile Squad in Gibraltar. He was not to return to England until January 1945, not having seen his wife and two children for 30 months. According to the diaries, which he continued to keep during this period, he arrived at Chatham during the late afternoon, where his wife, Winnie, met him at the railway station. After a brief reunion, he was back at work in Chatham dockyard early the following morning. Not even a day's leave was he permitted.

For those who had remained in Chatham throughout the wartime period, morale had remained remarkably high. Large numbers involved themselves in the various volunteer organisations; the Home Guard was particularly well subscribed, as were the ARP (Air Raid Precaution) and its allied organisation, the WVS (Women's Volunteer Service). With a headquarters' building at the Holcombe Technical High School for Boys, ARP wardens constantly patrolled the town, while canteens and refuge centres were supervised by women of the WVS. The AFS (Auxiliary Fire Service), open to both men and women, enabled numerous emergency

129 A reminder that a Royal Marine barracks once stood alongside Dock Road.

ON THIS SITE DURING 1779 TO 1950
STOOD THE BARRACKS OF THE
ROYAL MARINES CHATHAM DIVISION

This Commemorative Stone was funded
by contributions raised by the Royal
Marines Historical Society and unveiled
on 1 May 1997

130 Guns are very much a feature of late 20th-century Chatham. In Military Road, Riverside Gardens, the Paddock and the dockyard they are now seen as an essential piece of street furniture. This collection can be found overlooking the river, on the site of the former gun wharf and Marine barracks.

131 A pleasant summer's afternoon in late 20th century Chatham. Georgian and Victorian houses form a back-drop to Waghorn's ever prominent gesticulations.

fire stations to be opened, which units were frequently equipped with the Coventry Climax mobile pump and a hastily appropriated towing vehicle. In the dockyard, also, the numbers employed were greatly expanded, with 13,000 eventually working within its walls. Of these, 2,000 were women, undertaking duties normally performed by men as they had in the First World War.

The eventual end to the war was to hurtle Chatham into a new and uncertain age. The town had been created for the purpose of servicing the industrial-military complex, an arrangement that was to be virtually demolished over the next forty years. First to go were the gun wharf and Royal Marine Barracks, both considered surplus to military needs as the 1950s approached. The gun wharf, which was finally abandoned by the military in 1958, has as its chief remaining memorial the

Command House pub. This was originally built in 1758 and served as a residence for the officer in charge of ordnance facilities in Chatham. The Marine barracks, of which nothing now remains, was closed in 1950—the final parade of colours took place on 27 May. The pay and records office of the Royal Marines remained in Chatham for a full 10 years, in offices at Melville, the set of barracks standing opposite the main gate of the dockyard, which had begun life as the Melville naval hospital and was handed over to the Marines upon the opening of a much larger naval hospital in Gillingham in 1905. With the departure of this final detachment of Royal Marines in 1960, Chatham finally relinquished all contact with that particular military body.

The cruellest blow of all was the simultaneous closure of the Royal Naval barracks and the dock-yard. This earth-shattering decision was announced

132 Horatio Herbert Kitchener's statue, which stands opposite the entrance to Fort Amherst. It was brought to the town from Khartoum and unveiled on 25 April 1960.

133 The former galvanising shop which, in 1999, was serving as the dockyard visitors' entrance. Some 110,000 regularly pay to view the dockyard in any one year.

by Defence Secretary John Nott on 25 June 1981 and resulted in the loss of 7,000 jobs. It was a decision which flew in the face of logic, the dockyard having seen completion of a multi-million-pound nuclear refit centre only 13 years earlier, providing the dockyard with facilities unavailable elsewhere. The closure of this yard also ensured that a class of hunter-killer submarines was without a maintenance base. Attempts were made to encourage the government to reverse its decision, but a rather lacklustre local campaign made singularly little headway. The support of local MPs proved a mixed blessing.

The final closure of the dockyard came on 31 March 1984 with a poignant flag-lowering ceremony at sunset. Hundreds of Chatham residents assembled within the yard where they were briefly entertained by the Royal Marine band. As the flag of the dockyard was lowered on that final occasion,

many a moist eye glistened. It was a sad, sad occasion and an insecure future now faced a town bereft of its military connections.

Since the closure, Chatham has partially recovered. The former dockyard area has been divided into three separate and very distinct sites. The area around No.3 basin (technically in Gillingham) became part of a civilian dock complex, while the rest of St Mary's Island (also in Gillingham) has been developed into an area of low-density housing and purpose-built office accommodation. A third area, the oldest part of the dockyard, that within the borough of Chatham, has been taken over by the Chatham Historic Dockyard Trust. Here, a museum site focusing on the history of the yard has been painstakingly developed. Unfortunately, the Trust has been unable to attract enough visitors to make the project pay, and with no more than 110,000

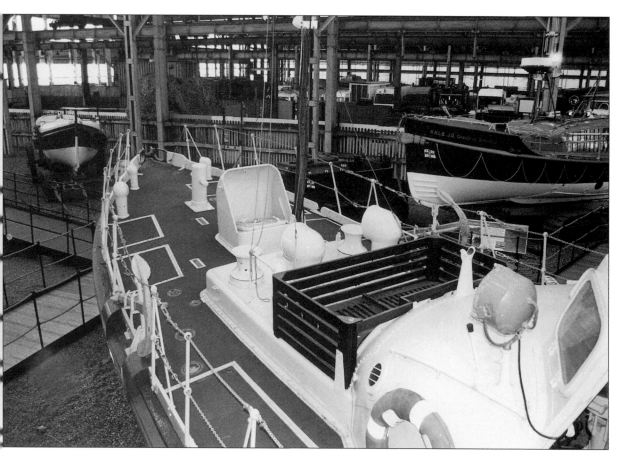

134 One of the major dockyard visitor attractions is an exhibition dedicated to the Royal National Lifeboat Institute.

ticket buyers entering the yard each year, there has been little chance to expand. In a somewhat desperate effort to double this number, the Trust has decided to investigate a 'fun' approach to dockyard history. Some of the proposed ideas give it the appearance of a theme park, with fairground rides and boot fairs occasionally reinforcing the notion that money speaks louder than history.

The town of Chatham too has witnessed huge changes since the ending of the Second World War. Many of the small terraced houses that once separated the High Street from the Brook have been removed. Such well-remembered thoroughfares as George Street, Avondale Terrace and Fair Row have long since ceased to exist, buried under Mountbatten House and the Pentagon, and few years later the High Street was pedestrianised. In the mid-1980s the whole town was carved up by

135 An unusual aspect of Chatham is its temporary library building. Replacing the original free library that stood in New Road, the temporary building has gained an amazing permanency.

136 The original borough library building immediately prior to its demolition in 1984.

137 The dream that failed. Those who regularly pass under the ring road will be forgiven for their sniggers when comparing the reality of the original proposal with the subsequent outcome.

a new ring road that allows all vehicular traffic to enjoy an extended circuit of the 'downtown ville'.

With final acceptance that the way forward was through creation of a unified authority, the Chatham borough pioneers, George Church, Adam Stigant and George Winch, got their dream in 1998. In that year, Chatham, Rochester and Gillingham were finally unified. At last, education, roads and planning have been united under the newly formed Medway City Council. As the nation enters the third millennium of the Christian age, this authority will usefully address the serious issues that have been allowed to persist. It is hoped that attention will be given to the crisis of pollution, the continuing excess of town traffic, under-funded education and the lack of open-field green areas. Surely the people of Chatham deserve a smooth ride into the future—for the ride through the past, most assuredly, has been of the white-knuckle variety.

138 In earlier years the High Street was a place of considerable character. Although there are obvious advantages in its pedestrianisation, the shops are those to be found in any other town. The Emporium of George Church and other locally run concerns have now mainly disappeared.

Appendix

Chatham Vicars, 1285–1568

Robert de Luda	1285	John Kynge	1568
William de Bordenne	1286	William Wheler	*c.*1587
Henry de Opecherche	*c.*1295	Robert Holland	*c.*1587
Nicholas de Chartiam		John Browne	*c.*1592
Henry de Apuldrefelde		Edward Miller	*c.*1595
Roger de Newenton	1319	Henry Ellis	*c.*1596
Roger de Wy	1332	William White	*c.*1597
Thomas Randolph	1333	John Deeke	*c.*1598
John Atte Welle	1339	William Bradshaw	1601
Henry Davyngton	1349	John Philipps	1603
John de Irford	1349	John Pyham	1603
Peter de Farleghe	1361	Thomas Vaughan	1635
John de Graveney	1362	Ambrose Cleere	1643
John Farleghe	1370	Walter Rosewell	1647
Henry de London	1393	Thomas Carter	1661
Stephen Gray	1395	Elkanah Downes	1663
John Marchaunt	1396	John Loton	1662
John Whytresham	1423	Francis Broomfield	1722
Thomas Vincent	1444	John Robinson	1722
John Maghefelde	1454	George Pratt	1722
William Ulling	1471	Walter Franck	1747
John Brenchle	*c.*1474	John Law	1784
Richard Gofredhurst	1485	Matthew Irving	1827
John Lawnscelyn	*c.*1502	Samuel Arnott	1857
Robert Aunger	*c.*1504	John Tetley Rowe	1895
Henry Merston	*c.*1507	Edmund Tetley Rowe	1907
Thomas Langley	1531	Frederick Wiltshire	1918
Lancelot Hollingbourne	1534	Aubrey Owen Standen	1929
Richard Longhorn	*c.*1549	Charles Augustus Herbert Lowe	1935
William Paynter	*c.*1553	Paul Randolph Shalders Nichols	1941
John Riddesdale	1562	Edward Ernest Maples Earle	1950

Lords of the Manor of Chatham

Godwin, Earl of Kent		
Harold, King of England		
King William I	1066	
Odo, Bishop of Bayeux	1087	
The Crown	1091	
Robert de Crevequer		
Hamo de Crevequer		
Robert de Crevequer		Also held Dover Castle
Hamo de Crevequer	1263	Supported Barons in the civil war.
Crown		Taken by Crown when civil war ended.
Guido Ferre	1291	Granted for life only.
Giles de Baddlemere	1330	Died without issue, inherited by youngest sister.
Mary, wife of Sir John Tiptoft	1339	Sister of Giles
Sir John Tiptoft		Outlived his wife and so inherited manor.
Sir Thomas Tiptoft	1367	Died without issue and inherited by sister.
Elizabeth, wife of Sir Philip Dispencer	1372	Sister of Sir Thomas
Sir Philip Dispencer	1374	Outlived his wife.
Margery, wife of Roger Wentworth	1423/4	Daughter of Elizabeth and Sir Philip
Roger Wentworth	1425	
Henry Wentworth	1478	
Sir Richard Lord Wentworth	1510	
Sir Thomas Lord Wentworth	1529	Buried in Westminster Abbey
Sir Thomas Lord Wentworth	1553	Son of Sir Thomas. Deputy of Calais.
Francis Baneham and Stephen Slanie	1566	
John Hart and Michael Barker		
Reginald Barker	1578	Monument in Chatham church.
Robert Jackson	1601	
Sir Oliver Boteler	1625	
Lady anne Boteler	1636	
Sir Oliver Boteler	1679	Grandson of old Sir Oliver Boteler
Christopher Rhode	1714	
Joan, wife of Christopher Rhodes		Given to daughter as a marriage gift.
Christopher Rhode	1754	
Charles Birkhead	1787	
William Coleman	1804	
Alexander Spratt	c.1806	
John and Alexander Spratt	1832	
James Best	1843	
Mawdistley Gaussen Best	1849	

Elected Members of Parliament (Chatham Division)

William Leader Maberley (Lib)	1832-34
George Stevens Byng (Lib)	1834-35
Sir John Poo Beresford (Con)	1835-37
George Stevens Byng (Lib)	1837-52
Sir J.M. Frederick Smith (Con)	1852-53
Lester Viney Vernon (Con)	1853-57
Sir J.M. Frederick Smith (Con)	1857-65
Sir Arthur John Otway (Lib)	1865-74
Sir George Elliott (Con)	1874-75
Sir John Eldon Gorst (Con)	1875-92
Lewis Lloyd (Con)	1892-95
Horatio Davies (Con)	1895-1901
Horatio Davies (Con)	1901-06
John Jenkins (Lab)	1906-10
Sir Gerald F. Hohler (Con)	1910-18

Chatham Division of Rochester, 1918-1945

Col. J.T.C. Moore-Brabazon (Con)	1918-29
Sydney Frank Markham (Lab)	1929-31
Sir Park Goff (Con)	1931-35
L.F. Plugge	1935-45

Rochester and Chatham

Arthur Bottomley	1945-55
J.M.G Critchley (Con)	1959-64
Ann Kerr (Lab)	1964-70
Peggy Fenner (Con)	1974
Bob Bean (Lab)	1974-79
Peggy Fenner (Con)	1979-97
Bob Marshall-Andrews (Lab)	1997-

Elected Members to Chatham's first Borough Council (23 March 1891)[19]

St John's Ward	St Mary's Ward
A. Stigant	G.H. Leavey
J. Breeze	C.T. Smith
H.C. Richardson	James Burrell
G.N. Whittell	George Clother
G.H. De la Cour	T.C. Lamb
G. Church	Frederick Perse
Luton Ward	
R.F. Brain	

Bibliography

Anonymous, *History of Sir John Hawkins Hospital at Chatham* (Chatham, *c.*1916)

ARUP Associates, *The Gun Wharf Chatham* (Arup Associates, 1975)

Baugh, Daniel, *British Naval Administration in the Age of Walpole* (Princeton University Press 1965)

Baugh, Daniel, *Naval Administration, 1715-1750* (Navy Records Society, 1977)

Baddeley, G.E. (ed.), *The Tramways of Kent*, Vol.1 (Light Railway Transport League, 1971)

Brayley, *The Beauties of England and Wales* (1808)

Black, Shirley Burgoyne, 'The Chest at Chatham, 1590-1803' in *Archaeologia Cantiana*, Vol.111 (1993), 263-80

Chalklin, C.W., *Seventeenth Century Kent* (Rochester, 1978)

Coombe, Derek, *The Bawleymen* (Pennant Books, 1979)

Coombe, Derek, *Fishermen from the Kentish Shore* (Rainham, 1989)

Clark, P. and Slack, P., *English Towns in Transition, 1500-1700* (OUP, 1976)

Cull, F., 'Chatham Dockyard; Early Leases and Conveyances for its Building during the Sixteenth and Seventeenth Centuries' in *Archaeologia Cantiana*, Vol.73 (1958)

Defoe, Daniel, *A Tour Through the Whole Island of Great Britain* (Penguin, 1971)

Douglas, James, *Nenia Britannica* (George Nicol, Pall Mall, 1793)

Dulley, A.E., 'People and Homes in the Medway Towns: 1687-1785, in *Archaeologia Cantiana*, Vol.77 (1962)

Fausset, Bryan, *Inventorium Sepulchrale* (Roach Smith, 1856)

Foster, R., *Chatham 100: A Complete Directory of Councillors* (Chatham, 1990)

Glass, D.V. and Eversley, D.E.C., *Population in History* (Edward Arnold, 1965)

Glover, Judith, *The Place Names of Kent* (1982)

Gulvin, Keith, *Fort Amherst* (Medway Military Research Group, *c.*1975)

Harris, Edwin, *Guide to Chatham* (Edwin Harris, 1912)

Harris, Edwin, *The History of St Mary's Church, Chatham* (Edwin Harris, 1913)

Hasted, Edward, *The History and Topographical Survey of the County of Kent*, Vol.IV (1798; republished EP Publishing 1982)

Howe, G. Melvyn, *Man, Environment and Disease in Britain: A Medical Geography through the Ages* (Pelican Books, 1976)

Jefferys, William, *An Account of the Fire Which Happened at Chatham 1800* (Chatham, 1801)

Jessup, Ronald F., *Man of Many Talents* (Phillimore, 1975)

Jones, John Gale, *A Political Tour through Rochester, Chatham, Maidstone, Gravesend &c* (1796; reprinted 1997)

Joyce, Brian, *The Chatham Scandal: A history of Medway's Prostitution during the 19th century* (Rochester, 1999)

Keen, Rosemary A., 'Messrs Best Brewers of Chatham' in *Archaeologia Cantiana* Vol.66 (1953)

Lambarde, William, *Perambulation of Kent* (1570; reprinted 1970)

MacDougall, Philip, *The Chatham Dockyard Story* (Rainham, 1987)

MacDougall, Philip, 'Malaria: Its Influence on a North Kent Community' in *Archaeologia Cantiana*, Vol.95 (1979), 255-264

MacDougall, Philip, *Murder in Kent* (Robert Hale, 1989b)

MacDougall, Philip, *Royal Dockyards* (Newton Abbot, 1982)

MacDougall, Philip, *Royal Dockyards* (Princes Risborough, 1989a)

MacDougall, Philip, 'A Demand Fulfilled' in *Southern History* Vol.19 (1997)

MacGregor, A. and Bolick, E., *A Summary of the Anglo-Saxon Collections* (Ashmolean Museum, 1993)

Marsh, R., *Rochester, The Evolution of a City* (Rochester, 1976)

Marsh, R., *Your Brother Still* (1953)

Morris, C., *The Journeys of Celia Fiennes* (Cresset Press, 1949)

Newman, John, *West Kent and the Weald* (Harmondsworth, 1969)

Oppenheim, M., *A History of the Administration of the Royal Navy* (London, 1896)

Perrin, W.G., *The Autobiography of Phineas Pett* (Navy Records Society, 1918)

Pope, Dudley, *Life in Nelson's Navy* (London, 1981)

Presnail, James, *Chatham: The Story of a Dockyard Town* (Chatham, 1976)

Rogers, P.G., *The Dutch in the Medway* (1970)

Salmon, Victor, 'James Best, Brewer of Chatham, 1744-82' in *Cantium* 3:4 (1971), 95- 9

Sandeman, A.E.N., 'Notes on the Military History of Chatham' (unpublished *c.*1965)

Smith, F.F., *A History of Rochester* (Rochester, 1926; reprinted 1978)

Waters, Mavis, 'Changes in the Chatham Dockyard Workforce, 1860-90' in *Mariner's Mirror* Vol.69:1 and 2 (1981).

Waters, Mavis, 'The Dockyard Workforce: A Picture of Chatham Dockyard *c.*1860 in *Bygone Kent* Vol.97 (1981), 79-94.

Waters, Mavis, 'Dockyard and Parliament: a study of the unskilled workers in Chatham Yard, 1860-1900' in *Southern History* Vol.6 (1984), 123-39

Witney, K.P., 'Development of the Kentish Marshes in the Aftermath of the Norman Conquest in *Archaeologia Cantiana* Vol.107 (1989), 29-50

Yates, Nigel (ed.), *Faith and Fabric* (1996), 39

Notes

1. On the Eve of Change

1. KAO P85/1/1. Although Thomas Cromwell, in the year 1538, had instructed every parish in the country to record marriages, baptisms and burials, these earliest records at Chatham have been lost. Possibly, they were kept on paper. As a result, the earliest surviving records for the parish date to 1568.

2. J. Presnail, *The Story of Chatham* (1976), pp.47-8. It is difficult to agree with Presnail's statement that these merchants were smugglers. The export of wool during the reign of Edward I was not, as stated by Presnail, an illegal act.

3. These storehouses will be subject to further discussion in Chapter Two.

4. The full story of the Cade rebellion can be found in S.B. Chrimes (ed.), *Fifteenth Century England* (1995). The full list of those from Chatham who were involved and subsequently recorded by the constable of the Hundred of Chatham is: Ricus Bedmynton, Willis Cooler, Ricus Cristyan, Stephus Cok, Simon Couper, Johes Chapman, Robtus Chelfield, Thomas Friday, Hamo Long, Ricus Lorkyn, Ricus Marchall, Willis Neel, Johes Pylcher, Johes Symcok, Johes Pery. Rogus Roper, Willis Short, Johes Smyth, Willis Thorp, Johes Tomme, Rogus atte Wode, Willis Warner, Robtus Wodear and Johes Wolf.

5. Presnail, *op cit.*, p.46.

6. William Lambarde, *Perambulation of Kent* (1570), pp.325-6.

7. Sir Roger de Beleknapp had acquired these lands some time around 1365. See N. Yates, *Faith and Fabric* (1996), p.39.

8. J.P. Hayes *et al.*, 'Report of an Excavation in the Grounds of St Bartholomew's Chapel, Chatham' in *Archaeologia Cantiana*, Vol.98 (1982), pp.177-90.

9. Lambarde, *op. cit.*, p.328.

2. A Dock Furnished for the Finest Fleet

1. M. Oppenheim (ed.), *The Naval Tracts of Sir William Monson*, Vol.5 (Navy Records Society, 1914), p.15. A cable was the largest size of rope and generally used to secure anchors while a hawser was of a smaller size.

2. PRO AO1/2588. Pipe Office Declared Accounts quoted in F. Cull, 'Chatham Dockyard: Early Leases and Conveyances for its Building during the early 16th and 17th centuries' in *Archaeologia Cantiana* Vol.73, p.76.

3. *Ibid.*, p.78. This would place the storehouses in the vicinity of the *Command House* pub.

4. Acts of the Privy Council, quoted in Cull, *op. cit.*, p.76.

5. *Ibid.*, p.77.

6. The bulwark at Sheerness was replaced by a fort in 1574. For further details on the Medway defences at this time, see M. Oppenheim, *A History of the Administration of the Royal Navy*, p.150.

7. The reason for placing mast timbers under water was that it preserved their natural springiness by not allowing them to dry out too quickly.

8. Hill House, which appears to have been constructed during the reign of Henry VIII, was a substantial three-storey brick building. It may be been built by one of the merchant traders using the port of Chatham. Surprisingly, little is known of this building other than that it was acquired by the Navy Office sometime between 1567 and 1581, remaining with the navy until the 18th century. Edmund Dummer, who served as First Assistant Master Shipwright at Chatham (1686-9), executed a detailed drawing of the house and this may be viewed at the British Library (BL Kings 43).

9. M. Oppenheim, *op. cit.*, p.50.
10. Raphael Holinshed, *Chronicles of England, Scotland and Ireland* (1577).
11. A.P. McGowan, *The Jacobean Commissions of Enquiry, 1608 and 1618* (Navy Records Society, 1971), pp.118–19.
12. *Ibid.*
13. Cull, *op cit.*, p.81.
14. Pipe Office Accounts, 2261, quoted in Oppenheim, op. cit., p.210.

3. A 17th-Century New Town

1. See P. MacDougall, *The Chatham Dockyard Story*, pp.23–4.
2. KAO P85/1/1/17. For some years it is difficult to gauge the precise number of births.
3. W.G. Perrin, *The Autobiography of Phineas Pett*, p.1.
4. The manor house at Chatham had become available in that year, the then Lord of the Manor, Reginald Barker, having chosen to live in a new house built on Boley Hill.
5. Perrin, *op. cit.*, p.116.
6. *Ibid.*
7. The specific days referred to were 20 and 27 July 1666, when 9 and 7 were buried respectively. It should be added that, at this time, with Chatham's population probably standing at 3,000, some 18 per cent died as a result of plague.
8. J. Birchenough (ed.), *The Compleat Parish Officer. A Facsimile of a 1734 Handbook* (North West Kent Family History Society, 1992), p.117.
9. *Ibid.*
10. *Ibid.*, p.179.
11. KAO P85/8/1, 5 June and 11 October 1643.
12. KAO P85/1/3, 22 November 1653.
13. Quoted in Presnail, *op. cit.*, p.137.
14. Presnail, *op. cit.*, p.111
15. Samuel Pepys, *Diary*, 7 June 1666.
16. PRO ADM106/309, f177
17. *Ibid.*, f190.
18. *Diary*, 11 June 1667. Pepys later blamed Commissioner Pett for the loss of *Royal Charles*, a first rate warship captured by the Dutch. According to Pepys, Pett should have moved the vessel higher up river 'by our several orders, and deserves therefore to be hanged for not doing it'.
19. *Ibid.*, 14 June 1667.
20. CSPD, Addenda, 1660–85, pp.193–4. Quoted in Rogers, *The Dutch in the Medway*, p.138.
21. A brief account of the Dutch raid may be found in MacDougall, *op. cit.*, with a fuller account appearing in Rogers, *op. cit.*

4. An Industrial-Military Complex

1. C. Morris, *The Journeys of Celia Fiennes* (Cresset Press, 1949)
2. Daniel Defoe, *A Tour Through the Whole Island of Great Britain* (Penguin, 1971), p.123.
3. PRO ADM110/12, 26 August 1741.
4. E. Hasted, *The History and Topographical Survey of the County of Kent*, p.194.
5. Brayley, *The Beauties of England and Wales* (1808), p.270
6. PRO ADM 42/166; ADM 42/172. In addition, the ropery at Chatham was employing 136 in 1719 and 70 in 1725.
7. PRO ADM113/5-10. By 1736 the number employed in the victualling yard had fallen to 47.
8. KAO P85/8/2, 21 October 1724. In addition, six trustees were appointed to oversee the purchase of land upon which the workhouse would eventually stand.
9. *Ibid.*
10. *Ibid.*, 20 March 1726
11. *Ibid.*, 6 March 1725
12. Anon, *History of Sir John Hawkins Hospital at Chatham*, p.12
13. A multiplier of 4 has sometimes been used. See, in particular, D.E.C. Eversley, 'A Survey of Population

in an Area of Worcestershire from 1660 to 1850 on the Basis of Parish Registers' in Glass and Eversley, *Population in History* (1965).

14. KAO, Q/RTh, 1665.
15. In the year 1726, the poor rate returns revealed a total of 1,131 households in Chatham, suggesting a population of 5,600.
16. KAO P85/1/77.
17. D. Baugh, *Naval Administration, 1715-1750* (1965), p.264.
18. KAO, P85/1/77.
19. In August 1772, the total employed at Chatham dockyard was 1,566, and it was to rise to 1,609 during the following year. In August 1785, the number employed stood at 1,614 and remained above 1,600 throughout the peacetime period 1783 to 1793. NMM ADM/B/186-200 and ADM/BP/1-20.
20. A total of more than 2,000 labourers and artisans employed at Chatham dockyard was first exceeded in 1799. NMM ADM/BP/19-20.
21. Between 1760 and 1815 the barracks was usually occupied by one or two infantry regiments (regular or militia). Among specific regiments were:

1772-7	Two companies of Foot Artillery
1783-4	Hessian Troops
1783-1806	Two companies of Foot Artillery
1787-1806	The Chatham Company, Royal Military Artificers.

22. A.E.N. Sandeman, 'Notes on the Military History of Chatham' (*c*.1965), p.4.
23. *Ibid*.
24. Arup Associates, *The Gun Wharf Chatham* (1975), p.45.
25. Evidence for the existence of prostitution at Chatham is implicit rather than explicit. Unlike Portsmouth, which had a notorious reputation, few have chosen to dwell on its precise extensiveness. A general account of prostitution in dockyard towns is contained in Pope, *Life in Nelson's Navy* (1981). It is also likely that wives and daughters of dockyard workers were also caught up in this trade. That dockyard workers condoned prostitution can be seen by reference to a report made by the Sheerness commissioner, who complained about yard workers keeping gin shops in their quarters and being visited by prostitutes. See *Mariner's Mirror* Vol.36:1, p.92.

5. Town Improvements

1. The Amherst redoubt was named after Field Marshal Lord Amherst (1717-97). Amherst gained famed as commander of the successful expedition against the French in Canada (1758).
2. Keith Gulvin and others have referred to this building as a villa with its precise location described as adjoining 'the reservoir wall to the right of the hornwork casement'. See Gulvin, *Fort Amherst* (*c*.1975), p.6.
3. In his history of Chatham, Presnail (1952) states the name Chatham to have devolved from the Jutish tribe of Ceatta whom he describes as 'a virile and numerous war band'. Such a conclusion is reached by remembering that the earliest known spelling of the village name was Cetham (A.D.880), followed by Caetham (A.D.975). An alternative to Presnail's suggestion is given by Glover (1982) who suggests that Chatham is a derived from the words 'Cet' meaning forest and 'ham' meaning settlement and suggesting that this area of North Kent was once thickly forested.
4. B. Fausset, *Inventorium Sepulchrale*. Fausset's comparable collection of Kentish Anglo-Saxon artifacts was assembled a few decades before Douglas's. His notes were not published until much later.
5. The Roman numbers in brackets refer to the tumulus designation provided by Douglas in his description of these finds.
6. Upon the death of Douglas, his collection of artifacts passed to his widow before being acquired by the Hoare family. It was Sir Richard Colt Hoare who donated the collection to the Ashmolean Museum.
7. Hasted, *op. cit.* p.193.
8. KAO P85/8/2, 11 November 1722, f29.
9. Hasted, *op. cit.*, p.194.
10. As there was considered no immediate need to enlarge the workhouse, this money was temporarily put into stocks and the resulting profits used to help fund the poor rate.
11. KAO P85/8/3, 11 September 1746.

12. The Zion Chapel appears to have existed from 1785 to 1837, and the Ebenezer Chapel between 1772 and 1823. For this information I am indebted to Beryl Payne.

13. For information on the census, printed returns, held in the Guildhall Library, have been used. The figures from 1801 to 1841 are given below:

1801	10,505	1821	14,754
1811	12,652	1831	16,485
1841			18,962

The 1801 census provides a breakdown of how the civilian population of Chatham was employed and showed that 1,244 families gained their main source of income from trade and manufacture (mostly the naval and military facilities) while 92 families were dependent on farming.

14. KAO P85 series.

15. *Ibid.*

16. NMM ADM/B/189–ADM/BP/15.

17. Jones (1997), 8.

18. *Kentish Chronicle*, 3 April 1795.

19. NMM CHA/L/30, 23 December 1792.

20. NMM CHA/L/30, 2 December 1792.

21. At that time there were six naval dockyards in England and these, together with the numbers each employed during December 1799 given in parentheses, are as follows: Portsmouth (2,867), Plymouth (2,830), Chatham (2,037), Deptford (1,382), Woolwich (1,357) and Sheerness (965). At the Chatham victualling yard in 1801, the number employed, including officers and clerks, was 146. NMM ADM/BP/20a, 2 April 1800; PRO ADM113/22, 30 June 801.

22. ADM/BP/21a, 1 April 1801.

6. Our Parish

1. William Jefferys, *An Account of the Fire Which Happened in Chatham 1800* (1801), pp.91-103. Jefferys, attorney at law, also served as secretary to the committee that was set up to help collect money to relieve those who had suffered as a result of the fire.

2. *Ibid.*, pp.97-8.

3. *Ibid.*, pp.91-3.

4. KAO U480 T1-8.

5. Hasted, *op. cit.*, p.199.

6. P. MacDougall, 'Somerset Place to Whitehall' (UKC, Ph.D. thesis, 1994).

7. Hasted, *op. cit.*, p.218.

8. *Ibid.*, p.219.

9. *Kentish Gazette*, 17 March 1820, 4d.

10. Charles Dickens, *Uncommercial Traveller*, Ch.XII. A further description of this area of Chatham, based on Dickens's childhood memories, can be found in his selection of writings entitled *Our Parish*. In this he writes of various neighbours, the town fire engine and the beadle of the workhouse.

11. Charles Dickens, *Great Expectations*, Ch.XII.

12. The names of these streets, all of which still exist and which were named after members of the Best family, are as follows: Best Street, Richard Street, James Street, Rhode Street and Clover Street.

13. Hasted, *op. cit.* (1798), p.193

7. A Town of Disease and Squalor

1. Major M.L. Ferrar (ed.), *The Diary of Colour-Sergeant George Calladine* (London, 1922).

2. According to the 1854 Board of Health report, samples of drinking water taken from the Medway always contained a yellow deposit.

3. *Rochester Gazette and Weekly Advertiser*, 3 July 1832, 4d.

4. PRO ADM1/3794. Memorial to the Admiralty sent by Dr Burnett. More information on William Burnett and the Chatham typhus epidemic will be found in P. MacDougall, 'The Chatham Gaol Fever Epidemic of 1814' in *Bygone Kent* 13:10 (Oct 1992).

5. *Ibid.*

6. *Ibid.*

7. For further information on Melville Hospital, see P. MacDougall, 'The Building of Melville Naval Hospital' in *Bygone Kent* 12: (Aug 1991).

8. *Rochester Gazette*, 18 October 1831, 4c.

9. Robert Dadd subsequently died at Cobham in 1843 when he was killed by his son Richard. Richard Dadd had been born in Chatham in 1817 and had subsequently achieved fame as an up-and-coming artist. However, following a tour of Egypt, he had become insane and slaughtered his father apparently as a result of this insanity. For further details see MacDougall, *Murder in Kent*.

10. *Rochester Gazette*, 19 June 1832, 4d.

11. For information on William Cuffay I am indebted to Bruce Aubry and Colin Allen. The Chartist movement itself had little impact in Chatham. Those drawn to Chartism were primarily employed in trades threatened by technological advances. This excluded those in the naval yards.

12. The ground for this cemetery was donated to the parish by the Ordnance Board. The old town cemetery, being within the grounds of St Mary's church, had become overcrowded.

13. The religious census of 1851 (PRO HO 129/54) records the following centres of religious worship existing within the parish of Chatham during the last weekend of March 1851: St Mary's, the parish church (rebuilt 1788), St John's (1821), Jewish Synagogue, High Street (*c*.1751), Wesleyan Chapel, Ordnance Place (1822), Enon Particular Baptist Chapel (1843), General Baptist Chapel, Hamond Hill (rebuilt 1802), Melville Hospital Chapel (1828), Christchurch, Luton (1843), Dockyard Chapel (1808), Salem Wesleyan Chapel, Rhode Street (1822), Wesleyan Chapel, The Brook (1846), Primitive Methodist Chapel, Fair Row (1849), Ebenezer Congregational Chapel, Clover Street (late 18th century), Chapel Hill Sunday School and Chapel (1812), Sly-Kate's Hill Congregational Chapel (1818), Zion Baptist Chapel, Clover Street (late 18th century), Catholic and Apostolic Church (1836), New Christ Church, Best Street (*c*.1801), Bible Christian Chapel, Union Street (1829) and Luton (1834).

14. *Chatham News*, 2 December 1868.

15. Children in the care of the Medway Union might occasionally receive bread and milk for breakfast and supper, while the aged and infirm had meat pudding in lieu of bread and cheese on one or two days per week. In addition, bread and cheese were handed out at the gate to travelling paupers.

16. PRO MH12/5250; *East Kent Guardian*, 28 May 1842.

17. PRO MH12/5251.

18. PRO MH12/5252, 27 June 1848.

19. PRO MH12/5252, 27 June, 20 July 1849; *Maidstone Journal and Kent Advertiser*, 31 May 1842.

20. For information on the Contagious Diseases Acts of 1866, 1868 and 1869 I am indebted to Brian Joyce. Much of his research has now been published; see Joyce, *The Chatham Scandal*.

21. St Bartholomew's Hospital, which lay just within the bounds of Rochester, was a charity hospital opened in 1863.

8. Incorporation

1. G., Phillips-Bevan, *Handbook to the County of Kent* (1876), pp.33-4, quoted in Joyce, *op. cit.*

2. *Chatham Observer*, 1868.

3. *Chatham Observer*, 21 October 1882, 2a.

4. A coal whipper was an unskilled labourer employed in raising coal from the hold of a ship.

5. *Chatham Observer*, 26 November 1881, 2b.

6. *Ibid.*

7. As already noted, the local town police could call upon the assistance of the military police as well as a separate dockyard force. At the time of the riots involving men from the *Constance* and *Linnet*, the local press called for a naval picket to parade the town when the crews of naval warships were given leave.

8. The new St Bartholomew's Hospital lay just within the parish of Chatham and was opened in 1863, with later extensions provided by a number of private donations.

9. Joyce *op. cit.*, p.16, quoted from the *Chatham News*, 1908.

10. The combined population for the Medway area in 1881 stood at 66,818, whereas the population for Chatham on its own was 26,525 and insufficient to acquire county status without amalgamation.

11. *Chatham and Rochester Observer*, 13 December 1890, 8d.

12. Frederick Stigant was the son of the Adam Stigant who had been active in the Incorporation campaign.

Having undertaken a legal training, F. Stigant had succeeded George Church as Clerk on the Chatham Board of Health.

13. This weighbridge, which stood at the end of Globe Lane and near the Paddock, was primarily for the use of merchants and local farmers. Those wishing to make use of the weighbridge would be charged at the rate of 2d. per head of cattle, 1d. for every five sheep, and 2d. per ton of goods of any other description.

14. The Salvation Army home, which had been opened at the west end of the High Street in 1883, was housed in a former pub, the *Oxford*. This had once been the most notorious of the High Street pubs, having a long association with prostitution and petty crime.

15. *Chatham Observer*, 24 Sept 1887. Re-quoted in Mavis Waters (1983), 169.

16. Information on the two campaigns led by Kingsland and Lewington are to be found in Waters, 'Dockyard and Parliament'.

17. Rod Helps, 'W.J. Lewington: Medway Agitator' in *Bygone Kent* Vol.14:2 (1993), p.87. Further information on Lewington can be found in a letter by Dave Turner in *Bygone Kent* Vol.14:3, pp.182-3.

18. Davies first won the Chatham constituency in 1895, receiving 4,062 votes. His Liberal opponent had received 3,499 votes. In fact, the Conservatives had won the seat in each of the contested elections since 1874.

19. R. Foster, *Chatham 100: A Complete Directory of Councillors*, p.6.

9. Into the Twentieth Century

1. At the time the company carried the rather cumbersome, title of 'Rochester, Chatham, Gillingham & District Electric Railways Co. Ltd.' This was changed in August 1899. See Baddeley, *The Tramways of Kent*, p.59.

2. E. Harris, *Guide to Chatham*, p.15.

3. *Chatham News*, 20 January 1906.

4. Results for the two elections held at Chatham in 1910. January: Gerald F. Hohler (Con) 7,411; J.H. Jenkins (Lab) 6,130. December: Gerald F. Hohler 6,989, L.C. Bernacchi (Lib) 4,302, Frank Smith (Lab) 1,103.

5. The 'Cinema de Luxe', a small venture by later standards, survived a mere 11 years. During that time it underwent two name changes, becoming the 'Silver Cinema' and later the 'Corner House Cinema'.

6. For a full account of the loss of these three cruisers see Alan Coles, *Three Before Breakfast* (Kenneth Mason, 1989).

7. *Chatham News*, 17 February 1917, 3.

8. *Ibid.*, 26 July 1919, 4a.

9. *Ibid.*

10. And on to the New Millennium

1. *Chatham News*, 8 May 1926.

2. *Ibid.*

3. *Ibid.*, 6 November 1936.

4. Jack Lacey, 'Chatham Grande' in *Bygone Kent*, 11:10, p.610.

5. *Ibid.*, pp.612-3.

Index

References in **bold** refer to pages on which there are illustrations.